Lessons Learned from the Gullah Experience

Powerful Forces in Educating

African-American Youth

To Carol
Oorah mus kno dis
ya tour group was da bestest
ebba.

5-21-02

Kitty K. Green

Thomas J. Brown

Kitty Green

Lessons Learned from the Gullah Experience

Powerful Forces in Educating

African-American Youth

Copyright © 1998 Thomas J. Brown

& Kitty Green

Library of Congress Catalog Card Number:
98-92835

ISBN 1–891404–00–8

Published by

Brown & Associates
Educational Consultants
5472 Wingborne Ct.
Columbia, MD 21045

K K & G Enterprises
Gullah-N-Geechie Mahn Tours
P.O. Box 1248
St. Helena Island, SC 29920

Acknowledgement

Our most sincere appreciation is expressed to Dr. LaVerne Davis, principal of the St. Helena Elementary School, for providing us with some statistics, and an insight into the strategic planning, commitment, and supporting structures that helped propel her school from mediocrity to a position of prominence.

CONTENTS

Preface

This effort to enlighten and encourage our readers to become more knowledgeable about a vanishing culture holds forth the promise of becoming more than a mere source of information. Our intent is to produce a resource that is written passionately and, we hope, convincingly about the Gullah experience and its influence on people, places, and events in general, and on the Sea Islands of South Carolina in particular. Some of the ideas relating to family and group solidarity, the importance of education, and the fact that oppression diminishes oppressors along with the oppressed, are not only informative, they are instructive. If only a few of these ideas are thoroughly understood and their implications intelligently applied, new strategies for educating African-American youth and improving the human condition will emerge.

The Gullah communities of the Sea Islands provide living proof that the most essential requirement for communicating effectively is the construction of language that is mutually intelligible. Some of the most fascinating attributes of the Gullah dialect are found in words, phrases, and expressions used to communicate survival skills. For the human race, nothing is more important than survival. H. G. Wells once wrote that learning from human history becomes a race between education and catastrophe. This effort reflects part of our commitment to ensure a victory for education.

While we have documented much of the information and many of the ideas presented, no claim that our writing is representative of empirical research is being made. Our only claim is that we have presented an enlightening resource that should be of considerable value to parents, teachers, and others who may have an interest in learning more about the Gullah culture as well as improving educational outcomes for African-Americans.

As the title of this modest manuscript suggests, there are

some poignant lessons to be learned from our ancesters. The extent to which those lessons are not used to improve the human condition is exactly the extent by which all of us are diminished.

Thomas J. Brown
Kitty Green

Part 1

An Historical
Perspective

Scholarly efforts at accurately representing the essence of the Gullah culture are complicated significantly by the absence of written histories. Even the information gained through research in African-American archaeology must be viewed in terms of the problems presented for archaeological data in general. More specifically, artifacts provide the basis for inference about particular aspects of behavior, not direct evidence of behavior. Therefore, one of Theresa Singleton's contributions to *Before Freedom Came* - 1991, suggests that the interpretation of the culture of slavery based on archaeological records requires researchers to incorporate historical and ethnographic descriptions of those behaviors derived from both written accounts and oral tradition. Even with these enhancements, this information forms only a small part of the integrated complex of human activities anthropologists traditionally define as culture.

The source of the word Gullah is probably African, although its exact derivation has not been established. Some anthropologists believe it evolved from the word Golos or Goros, a powerful tribe of western Liberia. Others are just as emphatic in their belief that its origin can be explained as a linguistically transformed pronunciation of Angola. It is important to point out here that regardless of its derivation, the term is used as a descriptor for much more than the Gullah dialect. Quattlebaum, in the introduction to J. Gary Black's *My Friend the Gullah* (1974), suggests that the word is used in at least three senses. He includes among them its use as the name of the dialect, its use in a pejorative manner to describe broken English, and its use to identify a sort of slave that is specifically different in build and stature than those from Guinea.

Bettye J. Parker-Smith, in an introduction to Jonathan Green's *Gullah Images,* identifies Gullah as a designation used to describe a population of Africans who were taken against their will from the Gold Coast of West Africa and transported, with culture intact, to the coastal regions of South Carolina and Georgia. The fact that these Sea Islands were isolated from the mainland and contained thousands of acres of fertile soil made them geographically acceptable to South Carolina slave owners. Separated from the mainland by creeks, rivers, and marshes, access to and from the islands could be gained only by boat. Most of them did not have conveyance to the mainland, other than by boat, until 1940. These islands, numbering approximately 1,000, are situated between Georgetown on the north and Port Royal and St. Helana Sound on the south. They were so secluded that the continued importation of slaves after the Slave Trade Act of 1808 went unnoticed, or at least uncontested.

In the article, "The Sea Islands as a Cultural Resource," (*Black Scholar,* March 1974), J. Herman Blake suggests that slaves continued to arrive on the Sea Islands until 1858, fifty years after such activity was deemed illegal. By 1840, the Georgetown district was populated by approximately 2,200 whites and 18,000 slaves. Lorenza Dow Turner, in *Africanisms in the Gullah Dialect* (1949), cites a South Carolina Act of 1803 that made the importation of slaves from the West Indies unlawful. This same law also prohibited the importation of slaves over fifteen years of age from other areas of this country except under certificate of good character.

By strategically selecting their slaves exclusively from the Gold Coast of West Africa, the South Carolina slave owners were attempting to minimize ethnic diversity in their slave population. What they did not know was that some of the Gold Coast areas had secret societies that prepared Africans within a given region to protect themselves and their communities from outside invasions. Additionally, these societies taught survivor skills designed to help individuals and groups overcome the most difficult challenges they might face. Unwittingly, they were importing Africans who were far more sophisticated than they had imagined. Consequently, those importations that continued for fifty years after the Slave Trade Act of 1808, were instrumental in helping to establish self-sufficient slave communities.

The geographical isolation, South Carolina's insistence on importing Africans exclusively from the Gold Coast of West Africa, and the relatively small numbers of whites able to survive the challenges presented by life on the Sea Islands, combined to create a living laboratory for the development of a unique African-American culture, the Gullah culture. Clearly, it was not the intent of slave owners to establish a system that would be empowering to the slaves. In fact, their intent was to distroy any sense of self-worth and create, in their slave populations, a submissive and dependent people. However, for the South Carolina Sea Island slaves, the human spirit was strengthened by isolation. The history and practice of a self-sustaining community, which they brought with them from Africa, strengthened their commitment to group preservation and gave rise to attitudes of selflessness and pride that have endured into the present generation.

Those Africans, whose ancestry worship and spirit of survival laid the foundation for what was later to become the Gullah culture, knew from the very beginning of the atrocities that took them by force from their homeland, that they were equipped to maintain their culture. Margaret Washington Creel, in one passage of *A Peculiar People* (1988), wrote, "They possessed a proclivity for rising above their near-tragic situation for the sake of community." Discussions in the chapters that follow will detail some of the ways through which this unique culture called Gullah continues to influence people, places, and events.

Part 2

The Gullah Influence on St. Helena, the Pearl of the Sea Islands

The designation of St. Helena as the "Pearl" of the Sea Islands is one that has been assigned by the authors. From our perspective, the legacy of St. Helena Island continues to have a profound influence on the preservation of the Gullah culture and on the life styles of many African-Americans who have settled in the Sea Island region. Perceptions are neither right nor wrong; they simply exist in all of us. In consideration of that belief, we feel obligated to share some of the information that figured prominently in the formation of those perceptions we currently share.

St. Helena Island, located approximately 50 miles southwest of Charleston and 40 miles northeast of Savannah, is about 18 miles long and 5 miles in width at its widest point. In 1707, it became the site for the first reservation for Native Americans to be established in this country. After unsuccessful attempts by French and later Spanish settlers, the English began to inhabit the sea islands in the latter part of the 15th century.

After having established Charleston in 1670, the first permanent European settlement of the sea islands was established in 1698 on a parcel of land located near the current site of Beaufort. John Stewart, a member of the landed gentry, was among the first to be granted land (1000 acres) on St. Helena Island. For over 200 years, the only access route between St. Helena Island and the mainland was by boat. A bridge from St. Helena to Beaufort was finally completed in 1927.

The slave population grew rapidly throughout the South and particularly on the Sea Islands. This has been attributed to their proximity to a thriving Caribbean slave trade as well as to the area's emerging plantation-based agriculture. This rapid change in the ratio of Africans to white plantation owners and overseers led, in 1660, to a series of provincial laws that established a legal precedent for what African-Americans understand as racism. According to Winthrop D. Jordan in *White Over Black: American Attitudes Toward the Negro* (1968), these laws stated some major differences between the social positions occupied by whites and blacks. While white indentured servants typically were freed after terms of service ranging from four to seven years, the blacks' term of service was to be for life. The people of the Chesapeake colonies hold the infamous distinction of sentencing that generation of Africans and all subsequent generations of African-Americans to a lifetime of oppression. Although slavery was legally terminated with the adoption of the 13th Admendment, the institution of racism continues to flourish.

Since so many Americans labor under misapprehensions about the meaning of racisim, we felt it might be enlightening to include a brief discussion on that topic. In order for this discussion to have the impact intended, the concept must be presented in such a way that denial of its existence is discouraged. To help accomplish that objective, racism will be defined from a broad political perspective that focuses exclusively on power and oppression. This suggests a meaning, that when reduced to its essence, reflects attempts to keep power, control, and wealth under the auspices of the dominant culture in our society. This understanding allows our discussion to proceed without any references to bigotry, discrimination, racial prejudice, and stereotyping. These are some of the manifestations of racism that we all find offensive. However, if those manifestations were eliminated entirely, but the power structure and other basic norms of the American way of life remained unchanged, racism would still exist. That residual is the essence of racism and is reflected in practices that have been institutionalized in our society.

White Americans seldom critique what it means to be white and to recognize the unearned benefits that result therefrom. Consequently, they have created some rather ingenious methods to deny the existence of racism. This denial is based on a fear of losing the material and psychological advantages they enjoy. By engaging in denial, whites rarely come to grips with the agonizing reality that there are two kinds of racists. **Active racists** are those who openly engage in acts of oppression, and **passive racists** are those who sit quietly by and enjoy all of the benefits resulting from the work of their more active counterparts. What's even more agonizing for white Americans is the understanding that to be considered anti racist, one must confront those basic norms, and other arrangements of our society, that allow oppression to continue.

The argument, advanced by some, suggesting the existence of black racism in this country, is based on a misunderstanding of what racism is and how it operates. While there is ample evidence that blacks exhibit prejudices and engage in bigotry, stereotyping, and discrimination, they possess neither the political nor the economic power to oppress any other races. The mere existence of black racism, would guarantee unearned benefits for all black Americans based on nothing other than their blackness. All Americans can view that scenario as an unlikely turn of events. In this country, racism is practiced exclusively by white Americans or others who may be identified as such.

For 18th century whites in the South, the increasing number of blacks gave rise to anxieties regarding their own safety. This was especially true of the South Carolina low country where slaves outnumbered whites by as much as five to one. By 1708, African-Americans represented South Carolina's majority population. This motivated whites to exert more forceful controls over slaves. According to Drew Gilpin Faust in *Slavery in the American Experience* (1991),

7

Laws appeared forbidding Blacks to bear arms, requiring slaves to acknowledge their servitude and inferior status by wearing certain kinds of clothing, and curtailing all forms of black autonomy.

Some of the same anxieties gripped the whites of the Chesapeake colonies although the growth of the slave population was much slower than that experienced by the South. An attempt at providing assistance to plantation owners in slave control has been credited to William Lynch, a Caribbean slave owner, who reportedly made this speech on the banks of the James River in 1712. Parts of it were quoted at length by Minister Louis Farrakhan at the Million Man March held on October 16, 1995. Many people who were hearing this for the first time, were stunned by the thought that the minds of African-Americans could be enslaved to an extent that could cause them to do harm to one another. The entire text is reprinted here in italics to indicate the kinds of strategies used:

"Gentlemen, I greet you here on the bank of the James River in the year of our Lord one thousand seven hundred and twelve. First, I shall thank you, the gentlemen of the colony of Virginia, for bringing me here. I am here to help you solve some of your problems with slaves. Your invitation reached me on my modest plantation in the West Indies where I have experimented with some of the newest and still the oldest methods of control of slaves. Ancient Rome would envy us if my program is implemented. As our boat sailed south on the James River, named for our illustrious King whose version of the Bible we all cherish, I saw enough to know that your problem is not unique. While Rome used cords of wood for crosses for standing human bodies along its highways in great numbers, you are here using the tree and the rope on occasion.

I caught the whiff of a dead slave hanging from a tree a couple of miles back. You are not only losing a valuable stock by hangings; you are having uprisings; slaves are running away; your crops are sometimes left in the fields too long for maximum profit; you suffer occasional fires; and your animals are killed. Gentlemen, you know what your problems are; I do not need to elaborate. I am not here to enumerate your problems; I am here to introduce you to a method of solving them.

In my bag here, I have a fool proof method for controlling your black slaves. I guarantee every one of you that, if installed correctly, it will control the slaves for at least 300 years. My method is simple. Any member of your family or your overseer can use it. I have outlined a number of differences among the slaves, and I take these differences and make them bigger. I use fear, distrust, and envy for control purposes. This method has worked on my modest plantation in the West Indies and it will work throughout the South. Take this simple little list of differences, and think about them. On top of my list is age, but it's there only because it starts with an A. The second is color or shade. There is intelligence, size, sex, size of plantations, status on plantation, attitude of owners, whether the slaves live in the valley, on a hill, East, West, North, South, have fine hair, coarse hair, or are tall or short. Now that you have a list of differences, I shall give an outline of action, but before that I shall assure you that distrust is stronger than trust and envy is stronger than adulation, respect or admiration.

The black slave after receiving this indoctrination shall carry on and will become self-refueling and self-generating for hundreds of years, maybe thousands. Don't forget you must pitch the old black male vs. the young black male, and the young black male against the old black male. You must use the dark skin slaves vs. the light skin slaves and the light skin slaves vs. the dark skin slaves. You must use the female vs. the male, and the male vs. the female. You must also have your white servants and overseers distrust all blacks, but it is necessary that your slaves trust and depend on us. They must love, respect, and trust only us.

Gentlemen, these kits are your keys to control. Use them. Have your wives and children use them. Never miss

9

an opportunity. If used intensely for one year, the slaves themselves will remain perpetually distrustful. Thank you gentlemen."

While we have not been able to document the authenticity of this speech, the events of the time frame in which it is alleged to have been made increase its plausibility. Historian, Willie Lee Rose, wrote in *Slavery and Freedom*, ed. William W. Freehling (New York, 1982) that the Old South was actually engaged in a process of rationalizing slavery, not only in an economic sense, but also in emotional and psychological terms. Slaves were not to be dominated merely by brute force; instead, masters endeavored through persuasion, manipulation, and negotiation to elicit blacks' acquiescence to the conditions of their bondage. One planter explained, "Inspire a Negro with perfect confidence in you, and learn him to look to you for support, and he is your slave." Many planters labored under the misapprehension that the slaves' outward docility was a sign of their consent to and acceptance of the conditions of slavery. Nothing could have been further from the truth. The notion of slave docility was challenged by rebellious blacks like Nat Turner, Gabriel Prosser, and Denmark Vesey, each of whom planned large uprisings during the nineteenth century. Next, we will provide a brief description of some of St. Helena's crown jewels.

Brick Church

One of the most famous landmarks on St Helena Island is Brick Church. It was the first Baptist church erected on St. Helena. Situated on a small parcel of land donated by John Fripp from his corner plantation, it was built by slave labor shortly after the beginning of the 19th century. This approximate date, around 1812, was determined by noting the earliest dates recorded on tombstones in the church yard. The original structure was a wooden building which was replaced in its present form by slave craftsmen and builders in 1855. The balanced and clean-lined style was typical of 19th century architecture in the South. Brick Church is two stories in height with a gabled roof and symmetrically arranged doors and windows. Brick pilasters, which extend from the footing to the roof, project outward between the windows and on the corners of the structure.

Although this church was built expressly for white planters and their families, slaves were allowed to attend services there. This practice was common among many Baptist slave holders. The slave population used the seats on the side, the rear and in the gallery. When Union forces captured Port Royal in November 1861, plantation owners and their families evacuated the island. From that point in time to the present, the congregation of Brick Church has been exclusively African-American. For a period of about three years, (1862 - 1865), the Penn School held classes at the church. From 1884 to 1973, the church was leased for a nominal fee to its black congregation by the Baptist Church of Beaufort. Beginning in January 1955, the sum of one dollar was charged for a twenty-five-year lease. In July 1973, Brick Church was finally deeded as Brick Baptist Church of St. Helena.

Penn Center

The Penn Center is one of the Gullah culture's most remarkable contibutions to St. Helena Island. Support for that statement is based partially on what took place there, and partially on the lessons learned that continue to affect the education of African-Americans throughout the country. Established in 1862 by a group of Philadelphia Methodists, Unitarians, and Quakers as an outgrowth of the Port Royal Experiment, it became the first school for African-Americans in the South.

While there are those who would have you believe that the Port Royal Experiment was a benevolent act on the part of the Union army, it was, in fact, another form of exploitation. To suggest that attempts to sustain a reformed version of the plantation system is synonymous with attempts to prepare slaves without masters for freedom is slightly disingenuous. In reality, the Port Royal Experiment became an expedient effort to persuade these former slaves, whose legal status became "contrabands of war" to harvest crops of cotton and other grain that had been left standing in the fields.

In late 1861, the Union forces were successful in gaining control of the Sea Islands' coastal area near Beaufort, South Carolina. While the plantation owners fled to avoid submitting to the will of the Union forces, their slaves and other self-emancipated African-Americans stayed behind. By some estimates, as many as sixteen thousand former slaves inhabited the Sea Islands. Isolated from the mainland and from near-by plantations by the tidal inlets that interlaced the Sea Islands, they had lived for generations without significant contact with the outside world. Through the Port Royal experiment, the Union Army attempted to replace the system of bondage, under which African-Americans had lived for generations, with a system of voluntary servitude.

Herbert Aptheker writes in *The Negro in the Abolitionist Movement* (New York, 1941) that in January of 1862, General Sherman requested that the War Department arrange to provide suitable instructors for the Negroes to teach them the necessary rudiments of civilization. He also urged that properly-qualified agents be employed to take charge of the plantations and superintend the work of the blacks until they were thought to be sufficiently enlightened to think and provide for themselves. Salmon P. Chase, Secretary of the Treasury when the experiment was launched, expressed enthusiasm over the possible benefits that could accrue to African-Americans. While Chase did not gain prominence as an abolitionist, statements recorded in the *Niles Register* (November, 1819) indicated that he did not accept the notion that Negroes were fit only for a life bondage. He saw the Port Royal Experiment as an opportunity to demonstrate the capabilities of Negroes. According to John Hope Franklin in *From Slavery to Freedom* (New York, 1947) Chase argued that if Negroes could be trained by skilled supervisors, educated by experienced teachers, and given a helping hand by the government, the freedmen would forever refute the arguments of those who held that Negroes were suited only for slavery.

On April 15, 1862, Laura Towne, a teacher and physician from Philadelphia, arrived at St. Helena to fill the position of housekeeper and secretary to Edward L. Pierce. Mr. Pierce had been appointed as the project's administrator and established headquarters at Oaks Plantation on St. Helena. Ellen Murray, from Milton Massachusetts, joined the project in June of 1862. Together, they founded the first school for African-Americans in the South. The first class for eight African-American adults was held at Oaks Plantation house on June 8, 1862. Class size grew rapidly, and soon the number of students (adults and children) had reached forty-seven. Having outgrown the available space at Oaks Plantation house, the school's founders made arrangements for classes to be held at Brick Church where as many as 110 students soon were attending. For three years, Brick Church was the site for these classes.

In October, 1862, the project's first and only African-American teacher arrived on the scene. Charlotte L. Forten, a free black woman from Philadelphia, earned her teaching certificate from the State Normal School in Salem, Massachusetts in 1856. Upon her graduation, she immediately became a teacher at the Epes Grammar School of Salem, a position she would hold for almost two years. In March of 1858, she resigned from her teaching position citing poor health as the reason for her resignation. The notice of her resignation that follows in italics was printed in *The Liberator* (March 26, 1858) as having first appeared in the *Salem Register:*

"We are sorry to hear that Miss Charlotte L. Forten has been compelled by ill health to resign her position as assistant in the Epes Grammar School in this city, which she occupied with great credit to herself and usefulness to the school, for a year or two past. Miss Forten is a young lady of color, identified with that hated race whose maltreatment by our own people is a living reproach to us as a professedly Christian nation. She is a native of Philadelphia, but was edu-

13

cated in the public schools in Salem. She passed through the Higgins Grammar School for girls with decided éclat, and subsequently entered the State Normal School, and graduated with success. In both these schools, she had secured, in no common degree, the respect and interest of her teachers, and her fellow pupils. She was subsequently appointed by the school committee to be an assistant in the Epes Grammar School. She was warmly recommended by her former teachers. She was graciously received by the parents of the district, and soon endeared herself to the pupils(white) under her charge. From the beginning, her connection with the school has been of the happiest and most useful character, disturbed, we believe, by no unpleasant circumstances. Her services have given entire satisfaction to the Principal of the school, and to the school committee, and have received their free approbation. We are happy to record this instance of the success of this lady as teacher in our public schools. We do not mention it so much to praise Miss Forten as to give credit to the community and to the school committee that sanctioned this experiment. It is honorable to our city, and to the school committee which appointed her. Miss Forten is hereafter to reside in Philadelphia."

In a commentary on the *Salem Register's* article, writers for the *National Anti-Slavery Standard* wrote: "The reader will not fully appreciate the value of this testimony to the literary ability and moral worth of a coloured lady unless he is reminded of the fact that Salem is the most conservative of all the cites of Massachusetts. Who will say, after this, that the prejudice against colour is invincible."

Since Fannie Jackson Coppin is usually recognized as the first African-American woman in the United States to receive a college degree, written history, has systematically excluded much of what Charlotte Forten achieved. This brilliant lady's accomplishments on St. Helena were never fully appreciated. However, for two years, she worked diligently to prepare the Negroes for a better future. Because the African-Americans were suspicious that those who wanted to help may not act always in their best interest, that lack of trust hampered the school's effectiveness. That fact does not diminish the commitment of these dedicated women.

The name, Penn School, was assigned to the project in 1865 in recognition of the generous financial support of Pennsylvania Quakers. During that same year, the school received its first two buildings in the form of prefabricated structures shipped from Boston. Using the expertise available, it required a full year for these prefabricated structures to be assembled. The buildings were located on a parcel of land, purchased from freedman Hastings Gantt , across Land's End Road from Brick Church. This site is also its present-day location. Although some religion was taught, Penn School was originally an academic institution stressing reading literature, writing, and arithmetic.

Dr. Howard Frissell, former superintendent of Hampton Institute, brought industrial education to Penn in 1900. Its name was changed to Penn Industrial, Normal and Agricultural School. This shift in emphasis, which remained until 1944 was planned to help the people of the island to become entirely self sufficient. The Frissell Memorial Community House, designed and constructed by students, was dedicated in 1925. The Tabby structure was under construction for two years. Penn served as a public school from 1948 through 1953. Since that time, it has served as a community action center. During the 1960's Penn Center played a strategic role in the civil rights struggle when it became the site of planning sessions conducted by Dr. Martin Luther King, Jr. and Andrew Young. Many of the plans for the historic March on Washington in 1963 were made at this location. The United States Peace Corps has used Penn Center facilities to conduct training programs. Today, Penn houses programs dedicated to enriching the lives of St. Helena's children, saving St. Helena's land and environment, and preserving island history.

When the Port Royal Experiment is viewed from a broad political perspective, interesting parallels between the motives and the lack of moral imperatives of the power brokers

15

of that era and those of contemporary American power brokers can be brought clearly into focus. What has remained constant is the desire of these power brokers to maintain control over the education of the oppressed. That sentiment was expressed openly in the *Mobile Register's* 1859 statement that declared, "We can have a healthy state of society with but two classes—white and slave." By changing "white and slave" to "oppressor and oppressed," that same sentiment can be identified as having influenced the major decisions regarding the Port Royal Experiment as well as many of the major decisions influencing contemporary public education throughout this country.

Praise Houses

Sometimes referred to as "Prayer" or Prayers'" Houses, these small houses of worship were used exclusively by slaves. Typically, these Praise Houses were crude unpainted structures of one small room filled with backless benches. By 1840, these modest little buildings could be seen on many of the plantations on St. Helena. Plantation owners, especially the Baptists, allowed Praise Houses to be built on their land as part of a sophisticated control mechanism. This would eliminate the need for slaves to leave the plantation to attend church where they could mingle with slaves from other plantations. Additionally, slave masters believed that Praise Houses would provide a risk-free outlet for slaves' emotions and hostilities. Some slave holders tried to exert control over the Praise Houses by appointing a favored slave to the position of Praise House leader. These same owners would attend periodically or have overseers attend to promote the slaves' understanding of the importance of obedience. While in attendance, their message was always the same; "Slaves, obey your masters."

From the slaves' point of view, the Praise House was not only a place of religion, but a kind of community hall where problems and frustrations of their daily lives could be aired. It was often the only place where slaves could extend and receive sympathy, settle disputes, find comfort, bond

16

with their community, and keep hope alive for a better life. In short, the Praise Houses, which were used by the slaves several times during the week, provided them with places to be somebody. Joining a Praise House, the American English translation of the Gullah phrase, "catching sense," signaled one's desire to participate fully as a member of the slave community. An adult or teenager could become a member by professing faith in Praise House beliefs, a practice closely resembling West African initiation customs. Any display of behavior judged to be unacceptable by the group could result in an individual's being barred from the Praise House.

Many Praise Houses used a bell to summon slaves to the meetings. In addition to the ringing of the bell, this oral invitation in Gullah, "Jine praise wid we" was often issued. Meetings, which lasted from one to two hours, usually consisted of preaching, testifying, singing, and shouting. The "shout," reserved exclusively for Praise House members, could take place only after the completion of all other parts of the meeting. During a ring shout, several people stood, sang, clapped, and gestured while others formed a circle and joined them. The steps were never changed, although the movements became more and more intense as the shout progressed. Feet were never crossed to prevent any similarity to common dancing. Praise Houses continued to be used after emancipation when St. Helena's churches became black. Many of them still exist and are used today in much the same manner as they were used 150 years ago.

The Chapel of Ease

The Chapel of Ease was an Episcopal church built in 1748 for St. Helena's planters who did not wish to travel to Beaufort for worship. While this magnificent structure of brick and tabby, does not present conclusive evidence that it was built by slave labor, it is represented in some of the oral history as one of the slave artisans' crowning achievements. Tabby, a common building material of that era, is made from oyster shells, sand, and lime. Lime is the major residue obtained from burning oyster shells.   Thomas B. Chaplin, owner of Tombee Plantation from 1840 to 1861, and the central character in Theodore Rosengarten's famous book *Tombee*, attended this church. The large vault in the churchyard was built for Edgar Fripp and his wife in 1853. He was buried there in 1860.

On November 4, 1861 a messenger interrupted the Sunday morning service to warn the congregation that "Yankee" ships were steaming past Charleston bound for Port Royal sound.   The militia, many of whom were present in the chapel, received orders, issued from the pulpit, to mobilize. The congregation left immediately to prepare in haste to flee the island.

The chapel was used for worship by freed slaves beginning in 1862 and continuing until it was destroyed by forest fire in 1886. For the past 100 years, the outter shell of the structure remains as a monument to what was and to what might have been.   One important fact about the existence of Praise Houses and the slaves' being allowed to attend Sunday services with the plantation owners and their families needs to be reemphasized. That well-disguised fact is that slave owners felt no moral imperative to help those in bondage establish strong religious convictions.   Their motive, pure and simple, was to create a more subservient slave population. Joyner in *Before Freedom Came* (1991) points out these important facts:

As early as 1831, The Reverend Dr. Charles Colcock Jones, one of the South's most prominent ministers, delivered an eloquent sermon urging slave holders to instruct their slaves in the principles of Christian religion. Not only would religious instruction save the slaves' souls, he said, it would also create a greater subordination among the slaves and teach them respect and obedience to all those whom God in His providence has placed in authority over them. Reverend Dr. Jones, pastor of Savannah's First Presbyterian Church, was also master of three rice plantations and more than one hundred slaves in coastal Georgia. His concern for the salvation of his slaves' souls may have been genuine, but as a master, he consciously and deliberately used Christianity as an instrument of discipline and control. He believed a faithful servant to be more profitable than an unfaithful servant.

St. Helena's Plantations

During the first 100 years of St. Helena's occupation by Europeans (1698 - 1798), the plantation houses were typically sprawling wooden structures to which rooms were added as the need arose. Most were porchless and located near the center of the plantation. Slaves cabins were built in front of the main house. These cabins faced each other and were placed on both sides of the street that separated them. There were stables, a garden, and often a family burial plot, all in close proximity to the main house. Each plantation had a road that led to a boat landing.

By 1810, planters became richer and plantation houses, which were built by slave labor, became more stylish. Most had verandas and were constructed near the water's edge to take full advantage of the breeze and the view. There were more slave cabins, but they were placed far from the main house as were other out-buildings. The slave owners' houses reflected the Beaufort architectural style, highlighting raised first floor, double porches, high ceilings, shallow-hipped roofs, and an orientation to the south or to the sea. Often, they were built in a "T" shape to provide each room with a view from three sides and more opportunities to take advantage of any breeze circulating. Typically, entrance stairs were doubled, conjoining at a platform just outside the front door.

Between 1845 and 1860, growing Sea Island cotton was so profitable that almost all available land was used for that purpose. By 1850, there were fifty-five plantations on St. Helena ranging in size from 80 acres (William Perry Fripp's "The Fending Place" to 1438 acres (Thomas A. Coffin's "Coffin's Point) on St. Helena Sound. However, most were between 300 and 400 acres. Ownership of the fifty-five plantations was distributed among twelve to fifteen planters. The largest land owner and slave holder was Thomas A. Coffin, owner of the Frogmore, Cherry Hill, McTureous Lands, and Coffin's Point plantations.

Part 3

The Gullah Influence on African-American Culture in General

What is most remarkable about the Gullah people is their ability to draw strength from ancestry worship and the strong belief in a set of values that places community at the very focal point of their existence. In truth, the Gullah experience represents the purest form of African-American culture. The retention of their African culture has sustained them, and their long identifiable lineage makes them unique among other African-Americans whose specific African connections are, more often than not, difficult to identify.

In the late 1700's, many Gullah slaves escaped from the Sea Island plantations and fled to Florida where they joined with Native Americans (Seminoles) creating an African-American/Native-American civilization. They prospered for decades as farmers until they were attacked by the army in 1835. War raged for seven years making the resistance of the African-American/Native-American frontier the largest slave rebellion to be recorded in American history. Finally defeated in 1842, these slaves were sent to the wilderness lands of Oaklahoma. They were considered dangerous and likely to incite other slaves to rebel if sent back into slavery on plantations. Because of the decision to isolate them from other slaves, descendants of the Gullah known as "Seminole Freedmen" still live today in parts of Oaklahoma, and Texas where traces of the Gullah culture and language continue to exist. One third of the people who traveled in the terrifying "Trail of Tears" along with the Native Americans between 1830 and 1842 were African-Americans. Ultimately, Oaklahoma was set aside to become a Black and Indian territory.

After emancipation, large numbers of former slaves settled in Oaklahoma. Many blacks who intermarried with Native-Americans received their promised 40 acres and a mule along with whatever oil was later found on their property. Through oil ventures and extremely successful farms and businesses, blacks amassed tremendous wealth and in so doing, figured prominently in a chapter of African-American history that, until recently, has remained among this country's best-kept secrets. The scholarly research of Ron Wallace and Jay Jay Wilson, co-authors of *Black Wallstreet: A Lost Dream,* found and compiled convincing evidence of what they now describe as "a black holocaust in America." Reference is being made to the 1921 massacre of African-Americans in Tulsa Oaklahoma. Recorded erroneously in American history as the Tulsa race riot of 1921, Wallace and Wilson chronicle what actually took place in Tulsa on June 1, 1921.

"Black Wallstreet" was the name fittingly given to one of the most affluent all-black communities in America which, on the date previously mentioned, was bombed from the air and burned to the ground by mobs of envious whites. In less than twelve hours, a once thriving thirty-eight square block business district in northern Tulsa lay in ruins. A model community of 15,000 residents and a major African-American economic movement was resoundingly defused. Not a single dime of restitution has been awarded the victims during the more than 77 years that have passed since the carnage took place.

That one-night's carnage left approximately 3,000 African-Americans dead, and over 600 successful businesses and social institutions lost. Among these were 21 churches, 21 restaurants, 30 grocery stores, two movie theaters, several law offices, a library, a bank, a post office, a hospital, a school, a charter bus company, and 6 privately owned planes. The impetus behind all of this was the infamous Ku Klux Klan working in consort with city officials and other sympathizers.

In their book and the companion video documentary, "Black Wallstreet: A Black Holocaust in America," the authors have chronicled, for the first time in the words of area historians and elderly survivors, what really happened there on that fateful spring day. In addition to presenting their opinion of why this bloody event occured, they offer an explanation for the recurring effect that continues to be felt in predominantly black neighborhoods today.

The largest non-military massacre of civilians ever to take place in this country resulted from the need felt by white supremacists to establish their dominance. The realization that blacks had lifted themselves from the permanent underclass, to which whites felt that they were pre-ordained, and had soared to positions of wealth, prominence, and power created envy and jealousy in a sector of the white population of Tulsa. Convinced that 300 years of bondage would produce values and life styles in Blacks that should forever keep them subjugated to whites was the trigger mechanism that mobilized the Klan and its sympathizers into action. It was reported that airplanes, some carrying police officers, hovered over the district dropping nitroglycerin on buildings. In a thirty-one page signed affidavit, information supplied by former police officer Van B. Hurley (white) documents the fact that prominent city officials and high-ranking police officers carefully planned for the use of airplanes in the attack. Hurley also declared that Captain George G. Blaine of the Tulsa police department rode in one of the planes contracted to drop incendiary devices.

At the time of this massacre, Tulsa was a rapidly growing metropolis of approximately 100,000 people. When the territory came into statehood in 1907, Tulsa was little more than a village. While the territory was highly profitable for agriculture, its mineral wealth was mainly responsible for the remarkable growth it experienced. In the fourteen-year period between 1907 and 1921, Tulsa grew into an ambitious city possessing the world's highest per capita wealth

(Tulsa Tribune - Sunday, June 5, 1921). However, the unequal distribution of that wealth resulted in a pattern that is typical of many cities today. Although Tulsa could boast of being a city of millionaires, it also had its share of indigents. The fact that much of that wealth was controlled by African-Americans was enough to push white supremacists over the edge.

A closer analysis of the black community of Tulsa reveals the strong Gullah influence on its culture. The concept of community was at the very heart of its existence. Shared responsibility for the welfare of other residents and for the education of each child were values embraced by the 15,000 African-Americans who lived there. By refining those survival skills that defined and sustained the Gullah culture on the Carolina Sea Islands, former slaves and descendents of slaves were the architects of a model community that was the envy of most of Tulsa. Growing fear in white supremacists that "Little Africa," as it was called by admirers, would become a prototype for black communities throughout the country led to its demise.

The Gullah experience also holds many implications for changes needed in public education in this country. The need for teachers to gain students' trust ranks high on the list. The marginal success experienced by Laura Towne, Ellen Murray, Charlotte Forten, and others who were committed to helping African-Americans prepare for a brighter future, can be attributed to the fact that these excellent teachers were not completely trusted by those they attempted to help. Because individuals earn the right to be called teacher does not ensure that they will be trusted to act in the best interest of students.

Erickson (1987) presents a strong argument supporting the necessity for teachers to recognize the importance of building trust and establishing legitimacy as essential dimensions of effective education. In an article titled "Transformation and School Success: The Politics and Culture of Educational Achievement," he states: "Assent to the exercise of authority involves trust that its exercise will be benign. This involves a leap of faith—trust in the legitimacy of the authority and in the good intentions of those exercising it, trust that one's own identity will be maintained positively in relation to authority, and trust that one's own interests will be advanced by compliance with the exercise of authority. "

Many African-American students, partially because of their socialization process outside of school and partially because of what they witness in schools, are hesitant to trust teachers who are white. Recognizing their political and cultural subordination, they often choose to withhold the trust that would allow them to engage in meaningful interaction with teachers. This suggests that in many classrooms, where white teachers teach black students, building student trust must become a high priority. Because building trust is an essential prerequisite for white teachers' success in guiding learning experiences for children of color, the challenges they face in culturally diverse schools exceed those faced by minority teachers.

Minority parents, even those whose lives are in shambles, view teachers as their children's best hope for a brighter future. However, if the teacher happens to be white, these same parents are skeptical about whether their children's best interests will be served. They very often see schools, in general, and white teachers, in particular, as part of an oppressive power structure. Since these concerns are discussed among minority parents, they are sometimes inadvertently and sometimes deliberately passed on to their children. This results in black children's entering kindergarten with a lack of trust in white teachers. In consideration of the perceptions held by Blacks, it is our conclusion that displays of care and concern for children's well being, demonstrations of confidence in their ability to learn, and demonstrations of respect for what they perceive as being culturally relevant are key teacher behaviors that accelerate building trust.

The trust building process can be accelerated by the use of exercises, designed to show teachers' concern for children as well as teachers' interest in students' concern for one another. Creative teachers, once they accept the responsibility for building trust, will find a number of humanly enhancing ways to accomplish that task.

The importance of the trust factor cannot be overstated. Some teachers have mistakenly confused their students' lack of trust in them with disrespect. While both of these concepts can be characterized as behaviors that undermine interaction that facilitates learning, their differences are clearly discernible. Disrespectful behaviors are usually displayed through acts of commission. As such, they should not have to be tolerated by teachers. Teachers have the authority to demand respect. However, behaviors emanating from a lack of trust are usually acts of omission or disengagement. Teachers cannot demand that they be trusted to act always in the best interest of students. Those who have earned the right to be called TEACHER deserve respect from both parents and students, but trust must be developed.

This discussion should not suggest that the trust factor is an issue which minority teachers can take lightly. The major challenge faced by this group is to convince black students that their trust has not been misplaced in them. Black students trust minority teachers until their trust is violated. However, many of these same students will not trust white teachers until their trust is earned.

The fact that the trust factor has such a powerful impact on the degree to which African-Americans become actively engaged in learning, suggests its vital importance as a component of teacher pre-service and in-service education programs. Our association with teachers and administrators, who received their education from more than 170 different colleges and universities, confirms our belief that sufficient emphasis on building trust is not now, nor has it ever been a high priority of teacher training institution. Lessons learned from the Gullah experience suggest its vital importance.

Another important lesson learned from the Gullah experience suggests changes in the amount of emphasis schools place on students' self-esteem. At least one well-known writer (Kohn, 1994) has concluded from his analysis of research and his own investigation that whether our objective is to help children become good learners or good people – or both – we can do better than to concentrate our efforts on raising levels of self-esteem. While this can be interpreted as a denunciation of the self-esteem movement altogether, such an interpretation is not representative of the position he has taken. His admonition to educators seems to carry a poignant message that should be clearly understood.

Kohn eloquently points out the dichotomy of thought engendered through arguments produced by proponents of two opposing philosophies. He asserts that those who defend self-esteem programs by arguing that children must feel good about themselves before they can achieve academically as well as those who bash such programs by arguing that children feel good about themselves when they acquire the skills necessary to be successful in school, have embraced philosophical postures that can compromise the primary mission of schooling. Both of these positions, as he sees them, argue against the notion that children can be taught in a manner that enhances self-esteem while dealing effectively with curriculum content. In spite of the absence of research that documents a causal relationship between self-esteem and academic achievement, his position seems to be a sound one.

Other prominent educators (Gilmore, 1982; Lazar and Darlington, 1978) contend that efforts to improve students self-esteem lead to improved academic performance. However, we now know that the mere coexistence of events does not establish a cause and effect relationship. In spite of this knowledge, school districts across the country are investing heavily in programs specifically designed to make children feel better about themselves. Much of this thrust to build self-esteem is fueled by a belief that many under achieving students will not strive for success until they can visualize themselves as potential success stories. Some of these commercial prescriptions may serve a useful purpose. However, the use of instructional time for their implementation should be examined carefully. In many instances, the return on the investment of time and energy is not worth the sacrifice of precious instructional time. In consideration of that fact, one might conclude that the most effective way to improve students' self-esteem is to explore that middle ground outlined by Kohn.

John Leo's poignant thoughts about the consequences of the self-esteem movement should be analyzed carefully. Leo's dismissal of the notion that self-esteem is a prerequisite for learning reflects his disdain for the growing body of "feel-good activities" that divorce children's feelings about themselves from academic success or failure. He suggests that this is why the obsession with self-esteem ultimately undermines real education. He justifies his position through the common-sense observation that exposes many individuals who feel good about themselves as not being worthy of emulation. He cites violent gang leaders, social snobs, economic exploiters, and high-living drug dealers.

William Raspberry (1991) asserts that what we want to instill in children is something that goes beyond self-esteem or dignity. He calls it self-respect. Unlike dignity, which can be accorded to the undeserving, or self-esteem, which can thrive on a diet of self-affirmation, self-respect is both an acknowledgment of personal responsibility and an assertion of one's desire to meet that responsibility. Raspberry contends that self-respect must ultimately be grounded in behavior. It is that set of behaviors, arising from obligation and determination, that drives the successful to become more successful and the unsuccessful never to stop trying. To stop trying is to lose self-respect. This can be accomplished in schools without sacrificing any instructional time.

Educators, may engage in semantic debate over the relative importance of self-esteem, self-affirmation, self-efficacy, and self-image. For which ever term they decide to use, the threshold condition for its existence ought to be accepting responsibility for one's own academic performance for which the obvious behavioral manifestation is striving for school success. The Gullah culture demonstrates clearly that even people in bondage can feel good about themselves. However, how one feels about him or herself is completely independent of ones desire to learn.

One of the most valuable lessons learned from the Gullah experience is that oppressive relationships are educationally debilitating for the oppressors as well as the oppressed. The variability of minority students' academic performance under different social and educational conditions indicates the impact of many complex interrelated factors (Ogbu, 1978; Wong and Fillmore, 1983). More specifically, sociological and anthropological research suggest that status and power relations between students and teachers figure prominently in minority students' school failure (Fishman, 1976; Ogbu, 1978; Paulston, 1980). Additionally, a variety of factors related to educational quality and cultural mismatch appears to hold important implications for mediating academic progress for minority groups (Wong and Fillmore, 1983). Two convincing examples of the powerful influence these variables can have on minority students' achievement have been documented by several different researchers. The academic failure of Finnish students in Sweden, where they are accorded low socio-economic status, is contrasted with their academic success in Australia, where they are regarded as a high-status group (Troike, 1978). Similarly, the Burakumin, considered to be outcasts by the Japanese, perform poorly in Japan, but as well as other Japanese students in schools in the United States (Ogbu, 1978).

The impact of institutional racism on teaching and learning should no longer be tolerated. As disquieting as its existence may be, teachers need to openly admit its insidious presence in schools and take steps to minimize its debilitating influence on students and staff. Although it has endured for ages, it can be eliminated from every public school in the country. The reason we have not accomplished that goal thus far can be attributed not to a lack of resources, but rather, to a lack of will. Teachers must choose whether to become a part of the solution or to be a part of the problem. Those who have the courage to become part of the solution, must continue to make that choice every day they hold center stage in the classroom. For those teachers willing to take that courageous stand, your effort may be hampered by the probability that many innovative initiatives, that hold forth the promise of interrupting the cycle of minority underachievement, may never be sanctioned for use in public schools. This sad commentary is not an indictment against teachers, but rather, against those who exercise a tremendous amount of control over the education enterprise. While we believe these "power brokers" exhibit extraordinary support for public education in general, they feel no moral imperative to assist in adequately educating all of our minority populations.

The rapid increase in minority population growth presents a serious challenge to those whose psychological and financial security depend, in part, upon the extent to which they maintain control over these populations. Since the subtle kind of oppression used by these "power brokers" is often presented as well-conceived strategies designed specifically to help those less fortunate than themselves, their influence on public education continues to flourish. A careful analysis of that influence may reveal interventions calculated to ensure that large segments of the minority population remain inadequately educated. A painful lesson from the Gullah experience teaches us that one of the most effective ways for oppressors to maintain dominance over the oppressed is to limit their education.

In spite of fact that most urban school districts have launched special initiatives, which focus on improving academic performances for African-Americans, Latinos, and the poor, regardless of their ethnic background, significant gains have not been made. Even more distressing is the knowledge that many successful teachers of these groups, who labor relentlessly devising strategies that work and who speak passionately and convincingly about the benefits for children that accrue from their use, have been excluded from the dialogue on education reform. We are suggesting that this systematic exclusion did not evolve spontaneously, but rather, through a well-crafted design.

The responsibility for removing this cancer from public schools rests on the shoulders of teachers. The job may have to be accomplished one teacher and one school at a time, but it can be accomplished. The reasons for its removal are obvious; the resources needed to accomplish the task are available, and the time to act is now.

Finally, regarding the implications of the Gullah experience for public education, those who have the responsibility for guiding learning experiences for children should be aware that some of the assumptions about teaching and learning, embraced by many educators, may be faulty. Since those assumptions hold the potential to influence your educational exchanges with youth, analyze them carefully and trust your own intellect when making decisions about their usefulness.

One such faulty assumption, held by teachers, surrounds the fact that some African-American students, refer to excelling academically as "acting white." The perception of these teachers is that these students willingly choose to under achieve in order to avoid that label. The fact that some students engage in this practice is a well-established reality (Fordham, S. & Ogbu, J. 1986). This should raise the question as to why teacher assumptions regarding the exercise of this behavior may be faulty. The fallacy in conventional educational thought is that these young people's priorities are so misplaced that they would rather run the risk of failure than expend the effort required to earn passing grades. Teachers arrive at this conclusion erroneously by making "acting white" and achieving academically analogous. From the students' perspective, "acting white" becomes the descriptor for the behaviors required to have noteworthy academic contributions recognized and acknowledged as such .

Upon closer analysis, this self-effacing behavior can be recognized as a rather unsophisticated kind of protest by students who are determined to hold on to what is exclusively theirs. They perceive the differential treatment extended by teachers to middle-class white children, to poor children, and to children of color. Teachers tend to validate the contributions coming from students, whose lifestyles more nearly approximate their own, and respond less enthusiastically to those of other children. Many of these students, who speak variant dialects of English, realize that their language, some of their values, and much of their way of life is not acceptable in the school setting. For them, "acting white" is willingly giving up part of the uniqueness of their culture rather than excelling academically. The clear message being sent by these students is we want to be perceived as excellent students, but we refuse to compromise who we are, what we believe in, and how we act, in order to be recognized as such.

This practice has become a huge problem in many middle and high schools with sizeable black populations. It has taken on a life of its own and continues to flourish because the efforts of teachers to mute its negative impact have been misdirected. Teachers continue to ask the question, why would any student deliberately fail to avoid being seen as one who excels academically in school? A more appropriate question to ask is, why these students feel that they have to "act white" in order to get their contributions acknowledged. To answer the latter question requires teachers to examine carefully, not only classroom dynamics, but also any teaching behaviors that may be at the root of the problem. To facilitate that effort, teachers should seek information about minority cultures from all available sources; verify the information obtained to form a knowledge base, and develop from that knowledge base a set of understandings that can modify many of the assumptions currently held.

Another area of the human experience where the influence of the Gullah Culture holds important implications for change in contemporary life styles is in parenting. The Gullah people's strong belief in togetherness made raising children a total community endeavor. More importantly, that coopera-tive process included the teaching of specific behaviors, skills, and concepts that prepared adolescents for adulthood. Certain rites of passage were withheld until acceptable levels of understanding and competence were demonstrated. This resulted in young men and women entering adulthood with a clear understanding of the responsibilities it requires. By contrast, far too many of today's young people are allowed to stumble into adulthood without the slightest idea of what being a responsible adult means.

While there are many things wrong with public education in this country, there are also many things wrong with the attitudes toward learning held by some parents. These parents, to which reference is made, are quick to point out shortcomings in teachers, school administrators, superintendents, and public education in general. However, a critical analysis of their parenting behaviors would indicate clearly that, for them, their children's academic achievement is not a high priority. Any progress made toward resolving the priority issue can be measured along two dimensions:

(1) The extent to which life-long learning results in parental growth that creates a stable structure for dealing with family issues; and

(2) The extent to which parents, teachers, and students recognize the powerful influence of intrinsic motivation.

Motivation can be thought of as the general energizing syndrome that initiates, sustains, and regulates various kinds of activity. While there are many conflicting theories concerning how it operates, the belief that it is a variable which affects learning enjoys universal agreement. Motivation to achieve can be used as a partial explanation for why some students excel academically while others, with similar intellectual endowments, never rise above mediocrity. One definite conclusion that can be drawn from the different motivation theories is, what might cause one individual or group to become highly motivated to achieve, may have no observable influence on another. Motivation is the key to unlocking educational success. The most powerful source of human motivation is understanding one's self. This may explain, in part, why the philosophy undergirding the motivation to achieve demonstrated by the Gullah people is *believe in yourself and draw strength from your ancestors.*

If and when this inner self is discovered, a hallmark of the Gullah culture, one's potential for learning is perceived as being unlimited. As this process unfolds, each of us is empowered to fulfill a vision of ourselves that surpasses by far any excellence goals embraced by public education. What's most important about this process is that it must begin and be sustained in the home. While its full fruition occurs during adolescence, the critical foundation has to be firmly established long before children come into contact with our system of public education. Those individuals who were deprived of the child-rearing behaviors that lead to the self-actualization of intrinsic motivation during adolescence, enter adulthood with few clues about parenting other than those modeled by their own parents.

Acting in mature and socially responsible ways does not come with age; it is learned behavior. The evidence suggesting that children cannot raise children continues to mount. Effective parenting is also learned behavior, and the models that have been presented for many young parents may not be the best models to emulate. Learning effective parenting skills includes, but is not limited to the following:

- Learning from unproductive childhood experiences while vowing not to repeat them

- Striving to grow intellectually, emotionally, and spiritually

- Demonstrating a pursuit of excellence in your chosen field

- Speaking passionately about education, and

- Demonstrating and extolling the virtue of strong moral character

Character development is an extremely critical issue because parents are its primary teachers. Since it is developed predominantly through the powerful force of good example, parents, teachers and students are all involved in the process.

Some programs, designed specifically to help bolster parenting skills, have been initiated by school districts and individuals schools throughout the country. Many of them serve a useful purpose. However, their impact on child rearing in general is negligible. One important reasons for their relatively insignificant impact on their target population is timing. In order to have a substantial impact, these programs need to be made available to couples long before they become parents. Once parents are caught up in the never–ending rigors of child rearing, the realization that they are neither emotionally nor intellectually prepared for parenting comes too late to change attitudes and behaviors that invariably lead to family dysfunction.

For those parents of young children, who realized after the fact that there were many things they should have done but didn't, don't give up. While you cannot change the past, you can engage in activities that will improve your child's chances for a brighter future. More specifically, you should commit yourself to all of the following things:

- Insist that your child is knowledgeable about the history of his/her ancestors and their successful struggles for survival (this is a tremendous source of motivation).

- Sit in on your child's class at least once during each quarter of the school year. Extending to teachers the courtesy of requesting a convenient time for visitations is usually appreciated.

- Make a point of meeting all of the professionals and para-professionals at school that have responsibility for any part of your child's program.

- Take your child to the library on a monthly basis. More frequent visits would be even better.

- Read to your child often and have him or her read to you.

- Initiate a conference with your child's teacher quarterly.

- Support school functions.

- Volunteer to help chaperone field trips.

- Ask questions about school and learning daily. This practice should continue even when school is not in session.

- Talk frequently with your child about the importance of education.

- Establish daily routine study periods for your child.

- Answer your child's questions and encourage him or her to continue asking.

- Limit and monitor your child's TV viewing habits.

If these bahaviors are demonstrated consistently, your child's chances for an excellent education are increased both at home and in school. When you, as a concerned and actively-involved parent, are convinced that your child's present school does not hold forth the promise of developing all of those skills and concepts that you feel are essential for a productive future lifestyle, you should examine some of the available alternatives to conventional schooling.

Another area of African-American culture that could be influenced positively by the Gullah experience deals with the sanctity of human life. Rituals of life and death hold particular significance in the Gullah culture. Charles Joyner in *Before Freedom Came,* suggests that funerals for the Gullah people were expressions of life's true climax. This is demonstrated through activities that reflect a religious ritual, a major social event, and a community pageant, all of which draw heavily upon cherished African tradition. Graves were often decorated with items representing or belonging to the deceased. Very often, the last item or items used by the deceased would become part of a monument to his or her passing. Christian slaves would thank God for the fact that the brother or sister who passed was, at last, free from bondage.

At the other end of life's spectrum, birth is also treated with a special reverence. Giving birth is a life-affirming act that bolsters the status womenhood. For this and other reasons, Gullah culture does not condemn women for giving birth out of wedlock. In that culture as well as in Africa, motherhood is one of the most important rites of passage for black women. Among the Gullah people, it is not uncommon for a mother to marry the father of her first child after its birth. The concept of illegitimacy, embraced by many in this country, is inconsistent with the African custom that considered a marriage consummated only after a women has demonstrated her ability to bear children. While this idea may be an affront to your personal values, remember that values are neither right nor wrong; they simply exist in all of us. However, those who perceive giving birth as the most viable defense against genocide, celebrate the birth of each child and willingly share in the responsibility for its growth and development.

One has to look only at the impact of black on black violence to understand the need for developing and nurturing values and behaviors that respect the sanctity of human life. We're suggesting that stronger connections with and a better understanding of the source of African-American culture can improve the human condition in many ways. The next section will deal with the influence of Gullah on many African-American's speech patterns.

Part 4

The Gullah Influence on African-American Speech Patterns

The "Gullah Tongue," is a descriptor applied to the speech patterns created by African slaves who were forced to invent a means of communicating not only among themselves, but also with overseers and plantation owners. At the height of the slave trade, the density of the slave population increased rapidly. By 1860, there were between four and five million slaves concentrated in the South. According to Jordan in *White Over Black: American Attitudes Toward the Negro* (1968), approximately ninety-two percent of all of the African slaves entered this country through the Sea Islands of South Carolina and Georgia. Out of necessity, a combination of their native language and English produced what has for years been recognized as Gullah. We will not engage in the debate over whether Gullah should be considered a language or a variant dialect of English. Linguists still do not agree on exactly to which category it belongs. However, there is universal agreement among linguists with the idea that Gullah is not "Standard English" spoken incorrectly.

Because Gullah originated in the South, it has some linguistic characteristics that are fairly common to that part of the country. For example, not articulating the post-vocalic /r/ (the /r/ following a vowel) is typical of many native speakers of that region. Words like {toe : tore}{coat: court} {poke : pork} (mow : more) are articulated in precisely the same manner. This suggests that the use of context clues is essential for mutual intelligibility in oral communication. If the sentences that follow were presented orally, the determination of whether _tore_ or _toe_ is being used follows from an understanding of the context in which the words are placed.

- *I tore my coat .*   - *I hurt my toe.*

The senior Senator from South Carolina is a well-known personality whose speech is a classic example of the typical southerner. However, because his dialect is considered to be regional, most Americans are not ready to conclude that southerners, who seldom articulate the /r/ sound following a vowel, have developed sloppy speech habits. Yet, the attitudes expressed toward African-Americans, who speak a variety of social dialects of English, are much more intolerant.

Of the four categories into which dialects fall, regional, occupational, personal, and social, Gullah and Urban Ghetto Speech (Ebonics or "Black English") are considered by some linguists to be social dialects. As such, they are associated with a specific cultural or social group and have become the targets of discrimination. Historically, social dialects have become the bases for more discriminatory acts than either race or skin color. A classic example of this is the ridicule endured by the Cockney speaker, Eliza Doolittle in "My Fair Lady." In the United States, perceptions of one's intellect, motivation to achieve, and level of educational attainment are based on how others perceive his or her command of "Standard English."

The bottom line is that there are many variant dialects of English that exist under the umbrella of Black English. All are legitimate dialects and have been recognized as such by the Linguistic Society of America. However, it should be pointed out here that Gullah, the authentic Black English, and a number of variant dialects of English known as Urban Ghetto Speech are not the same. The major difference between the two is that the Gullah people constructed language by intermingling west African words with English, French, German, Portuguese, Scottish Gaelic, and Spanish and by creating phonologically similar substitutes for existing English words to produce units of meaning. Urban Ghetto Speech reconstructs language by using English words in different syntactical configurations. These variant dialects of English exist in free variation and can be heard in many parts of the country. Unfortunately, all of the attributes most often associated with their use have negative connotations.

Gullah, like "Standard English," has undergone many transformations over the years. In spite of the absence of written histories, through which culture is transmitted, many of the original Gullah words have survived. The list of Gullah words and phrases, along with their "Standard English" equivalents in Figure 1, is provided to help demonstrate the semantic and phonological differences from most of those dialects identified as Urban Ghetto Speech.

"Dat Gullah"

"twixt"	between	"scade"	afraid
"whatsomever"	whatever	"needa"	neither
"oman"	woman	"fo"	before
"gwine"	going	"b'doubt"	without
"een ya"	in here	"ebenin"	evening
"kotch"	catch	"sot"	sat
"hunnah"	you all	"goffa"	got to
"day clean"	dawn	"doom"	do it

Figure 1

How teachers react to their students' use of variant dialects of English is a major factor contributing to students' school success or failure. Enlightened educators recognize one of the major premises on which the philosophy of culturally pluralistic education rests as the belief that differences should not only be tolerated, they must be affirmed. Nothing violates that principle more flagrantly than those strategies for delivering instructional services that demean variant dialects of English. In order to insulate themselves from ridicule, native speakers of these dialects are often reluctant to contribute to classroom activities. This is particularly true when they have reason to believe that those contributions will be judged on their conformance with accepted language conventions rather than content. However, the decision by students to remain silent often elicits teacher reactions that serve to exacerbate further an already dehumanizing experience. These students soon succumb to feelings of not belonging and withdraw completely from all learning activities.

Several strategies designed for use with students who speak variant dialects of English have been found to produce incredible results. These strategies allow teachers to take full advantage of what students already know while helping them acquire the skills they want to teach. This is accomplished without compromising either the obligation to teach proficiency in speaking and writing the dialect of the upwardly mobile or the kind of relationship necessary for meaningful interaction to occur.

Before either of these strategies is presented, it may be helpful to examine a seldom-voiced perspective on why our schools have not been more effective in teaching "standard English" to speakers of variant dialects. Probably the most significant reason is an outgrowth of the language supremacy mentality which mandates that most English for Speakers of Other Languages (ESOL) programs be taught exclusively in English. This total immersion approach, which runs counter to much of what we know about how children learn, continues to leave many casualties in its wake. Even very limited assistance in their native language would accelerate learning dramatically for ESOL students. Secondly, the teachers who recognize the benefits of taking full advantage of what students already know, have been provided with virtually no assistance in developing a systematic approach to the delivery of instructional services.

If students, who speak variant dialects of English, are to benefit fully from what schools have to offer, teachers' efforts toward that end must begin with acceptance of those dialects as legitimate means of communicating. Their legitimacy rests on the following facts:

They satisfy the requirement of mutual intelligibility.
They are systematic.
They represent, for some students, the only means of
communication known.

The two short stories that follow, one of which is true, are included to help establish the legitimacy of urban ghetto speech.

The first story deals with a zebra who went through life confused about its identity. The source of that confusion was not knowing whether its color was black with white stripes or white with black stripes. Having died before this dilemma was resolved, the zebra asked his burning question of Saint Peter. Saint Peter told the zebra to go inside and ask the Lord. When the zebra addressed his question to the Lord, the Lord's reply was, "You are what you are." Feeling uncomfortable about questioning the Lord any further, the zebra thanked Him for the information and returned to the room where Saint Peter was still on duty. Upon seeing the zebra return, Saint Peter asked if its dilemma had been resolved. The zebra replied by saying the Lord said you are what you are. Saint Peter said, well now, therein resides your answer. You now know that you are white with black stripes. The zebra was still confused, so he asked Saint Peter how he could be sure of that. Saint Peter's reply was, "If you were black with white stripes, the Lord would have said YOU BE'S WHAT YOU IS."

The second story is about a black first team All American basketball player who lead his division-I team to a national championship. Because his pursuit of excellence was directed exclusively toward basketball, his academic accomplishments left something to be desired. His communication skills demonstrated a lack of facility with "standard English." However, his basketball skills supported four years of attendance at one of this country's prominent universities. With the end of his eligibility came a multi-million dollar contract from a National Basketball Association (NBA) team. Within three short years, this young man was a dominant force in the NBA and one who many young black children wanted to emulate. Because the management of many of the NBA teams understands the powerful influence its superstars have on our youth, they encourage their players to visit schools and talk with students about the harmful effects of substance abuse. The general manager of this young man's team was concerned about the ability of this superstar, who shall remain nameless, to communicate with students. More specifically, his concern related to his lack of facility with "standard English." In a tutorial session designed to help improve the superstar's communication skills, the management was made to understand the legitimacy of urban ghetto speech. This happened when the superstar told his tutors that students would rather hear him say, "I is rich" than "I am poor." This true story helps us keep the relative importance of "Standard English" in perspective.

If minorities are to enjoy the benefits that should accrue from schooling, their culture must figure prominently in the learning process. Interacting with students who speak variant dialects of English presents numerous opportunities to test that theory. Unfortunately, far too many educators fail to take advantage of those opportunities. Teachers who campaign vigorously to eradicate the use of urban ghetto speech from school settings are not only fighting a losing battle, they are erecting barriers to meaningful interaction that are extremely difficult to remove. When students are told constantly that their verb forms are incorrect or that their syntax is awkward, they decide that the risks involved in communicating with teachers outweigh the benefits. This decision results in limited interaction with teachers and ultimately, limited opportunities to engage actively in planned learning experiences.

Teachers who possess an adequate understanding of the structure of American English recognize the existence of many dialectical variants. They also recognize that most native speakers of variant dialects speak them fluently and in accordance with the linguistic structures upon which they are founded. Because these teachers have reached this level of enlightenment, they perceive these dialectical variants not as "Standard English" spoken incorrectly, but rather as structurally different dialects. They convince their students that the push toward facility with "Standard English" is an attempt to have them acquire another way of communicating as opposed to a campaign to eradicate the one they are using. An effective way to accomplish this is through comparative analyses and progressive differentiations between the dialects under study. This requires that teachers possess a working knowledge of these dialects. When appropriate substitutions are suggested by teachers, students will switch codes willingly and with relative ease. Much of the success of this approach is realized because students see it as being additive rather than subtractive. The importance of the <u>ADDITIVE</u> as opposed to the <u>SUBTRACTIVE</u> approach cannot be overstated.

Teachers who embrace this method are perceived by their students as individuals exhibiting genuine interest in them and their culture. Those student perceptions help create and maintain the kind of relationships that support meaningful interaction. Teachers who are committed to the subtractive approach are perceived by students as individuals who are attempting to deprive them of something that is exclusively theirs. Against those odds, the most creative efforts by teachers to maintain relationships that support meaningful interaction are impotent. **When teachers can't interact with students, they can't teach them.**

Learning the variant dialect spoken by many children and adults does not require extensive knowledge of linguistics. It requires only the desire to learn and the personal investment of time and energy. This can be accomplished by most teachers, or other interested individuals, in four easy steps:

Collect speech samples of unstructured conversations in sufficient quantity to ensure that all the verb tenses used in the dialect are included. Pure samples must be collected, and they are most easily obtained from student conversations held informally in the cafeteria or on the playground. Samples obtained from conversaions between students and teachers are usually contaminated by students' attempts to speak in a manner thought to be more nearly acceptable to teachers.

Analyze the samples within the context used so that accurate meaning can be derived. When in doubt about the meaning they are trying to convey, ask the students. While "Standard English" is not a part of these students' expressive speech pattern, it is an important component of their receptive language facility. For many of them, it's their only way of connecting with the outside world.

Translate these samples into "Standard English" noting the differences in linguistic structure. If help is needed from the students, don't hesitate to use them as resources. They are the experts, and the fact that you seek their assistance increases their confidence in and respect for you as a teacher.

Write a grammar for the variant dialect. This step is extremely important. While the students can communicate fluently in many of the dialects you will encounter, many of them do not understand its grammar. Once this is taught, students are able to see that "He been done ate" and "He has eaten" may be grammatically equivalent.

Armed with this newly acquired knowledge, the possibilities for designing activities that accelerate acquisition and use of "Standard English" are limitless. For example, you can have students transform sentences, written in a dialectical variant, into "Standard English." Conjugation exercises requiring students to concentrate on variant verb forms and their "Standard English" equivalents represent investments of time and energy that pay huge dividends. Students participate enthusiastically, and the amount of learning that takes place in a relatively short period of time is amazing.

Urban Ghetto Speech, like Black English, is a generic descriptor used to classify many of the variant dialects of English spoken by African-American subcultures. What's most misleading about the use of these designations is the suggestion of the existence of one dialect. These variant dialects, unlimited in number and existing in free variation, have some common characteristics. However, it is important to understand that the number of verb tenses embraced and how they are used distinguishes one variant dialect from another. The fact that several common phonological features have been identified, facilitates the effort to switch codes from variant dialects to "Standard English." As one's under-standing of Urban Ghetto Speech increases, it becomes easier to develop a deeper understanding of and appreciation for the Gullah dialect. It was Gullah that gave rise to the variety of variant dialects commonly referred to as "Black English." Several of the common characteristics of "Black English," along with examples, are presented below:

- <u>Multiple negation</u> – – – – – – – – – – (She ain't never done nothing to nobody).
- <u>Verb defective</u> – – – – – – – – – – – (He in the car)
- <u>/l/ deletion</u> – – – – – – – – – – – – (fawe for fall)
- <u>Post-vocalic /r/ deletion</u> – – – – – – – – – – (mo for more)
- <u>Final consonant deletion</u> – – – – – – – – (fine for find)
- <u>Consonant cluster simplification</u> – – – – – (swiff for swift)
- <u>"be" or "be's"for habitual or enduring conditions</u> - (She be's eat'n with her fingers).
- <u>"been" for existing and past conditions</u> – – (He been eat'n with his fingers).
- <u>"done" signals action completed</u> – – – – – (She done exercising for today).
- <u>"been done" signals that an action was completed a long time ago</u> – (He been done finished his homework).

Just as African words worked themselves into the Gullah dialect, there are many slang expressions that worked their way into "Standard English." Unlike the many character-istics listed above, slang expressions do not alter the struc-ture of a given variant dialect. However, their presence fig-ures prominently in terms of mutual intelligibility. To omit their impact on the communication process from our dis-cussion would diminish the importance of the concept of mutual intelligibility. To bring its importance more clearly in-to focus, let's take a look at how culture can cause a simple event to be perceived differently by culturally different indi-viduals, and also examine several sentences that give rise to varying interpretations.

Two parents, one Asian and the other Hispanic, both decided that they would drive their girls to the bus stop and allow them to wait in the car until the bus arrived. When the weather was extremely cold, many parents would do this to protect their children's health. On this particular morning, an emergency vehicle had tied up traffic on the route these parents were taking to the bus stop. As a result of the delay both parents experienced, the bus had gone when they finally got to the stop. They drove their children to school and explained to the secretary why they were late. Both parents gave essentially the same account of what had taken place. However, the Asian parent said, "My daughter missed the bus," while the Hispanic parent said, "The bus left my daughter." It is safe to assume that culture figured prominently in the different perceptions formed by each parent. Below, we will see how culture can alter the perceived meanings of sentences.

Example: *The dogs looked longer than the cats.*

While this sentence is grammatically correct, in that it conforms to the writing conventions of American English, many native speakers of the language would perceive its ambiguity. The meanings derived might include the understanding that the dogs appeared to be longer in length than the cats as well as the understanding that the dogs spent more time in search of something than did the cats. However, cultural literacy and world view play important roles in the process of deriving meaning. Those individuals who perceive both time and distance from a linear perspective are likely to see the sentence as being ambiguous. Those who perceive time as being cyclic rather than linear are likely to understand the sentence to mean only that the dogs appeared to be longer in length than the cats. For those individuals, perceiving time as progressing in a linear fashion is counter intuitive. Let's examine another example that is similar in structure:

I'm going to check out some library books.

While the words <u>check out</u> give rise to ambiguity for some, most mainstream Americans would see this sentence as conveying a single meaning. However, many African-Americans and some Hispanics, depending upon where they live, would perceive two possible meanings: 1. **To inspect library books** and 2. **To sign out library books** In culturally diverse classrooms, the potential for misunderstandings to occur is enormous. However, in culturally responsive classrooms, those chances for cross-cultural miscommunication are reduced significantly. The final sentence for examination presents a different kind of challenge to mutual intelligibility.

The greenhouse is empty.

In this case, the problem of ambiguity is more likely to arise during oral communication. The graphic representation clearly indicates that greenhouse is a compound. As such, its meaning is clear. However in oral communication, the difference between the compound, <u>greenhouse,</u> and the noun adjunct, <u>green house,</u> is determined phonologically. The stress pattern for the compound is ´green`house while the stress pattern for the noun adjunct is ´green ´house. As you can see, the chances for miscommunication in "Standard English" are prevalent without the introduction of slang expressions. You can imagine how those chances are increased when the use of slang expressions is the rule rather than the exception.

There are those educators who will criticize any suggestion of becoming familiar with the slang expressions used by their students. However, the position being represented by these authors is that teachers who do not familiarize themselves with their students' slang are sacrificing opportunities to enhance student / teacher interaction. Interaction and content combine to form the quality control for the teaching endeavor. Both are affected adversely when two-way communication functions at less than peak performance. Following are some contemporary slang expressions along with meanings that are used with increasing regularity by many youth and adults. A few Gullah expressions are included to heighten awareness of the importance of mutual intelligibility.

- **Chill or chill out** – – – – – – – – calm down, relax
- **Give suck** – – – – – – – – – to breast feed a baby
- **Tripping** – – – – – – – – making a fool of one's self
- **Give out** – – – – – – – – – – – – – announce
- **Got it going on** – – having a lot going for one's self
- **Catching sense** – – joining a church or Praise House
- **In your face** – – – a violation of one's personal space
- **Fresh** – – – – – – – – – – – – – attractive or good looking
- **Hurry up and dead** – – – – – – – – die soon
- **All done away** – – – – – – – – – – over with
- **Ain't all that** – – – – – – – – – – – – – – not a big deal
- **Make do** – – – – – – – – – – use what's available
- **Smoking or smok'n** – – – – – – – – being real cool
- **Dis** – – – – – – – – – – – – – – – – – – – disrespect
- **I'm not about that** – - - – – – – Don't misjudge me.
- **You go girl!** – – – – keep doing what you're doing

When you're not sure what slang expressions mean, ask those who know. They will be delighted to explain their meanings and even more delighted that you've asked.

Before engaging in any of the code switching activities included in this chapter, we want to present some additional information about the Gullah dialect. It's important to remember the circumstances under which this dialect emerged. Survival often depended upon slaves' ability to understand when spoken to by overseers, and not be understood by overseers when speaking to another slave. This required the slaves to develop a receptive language mode that differed significantly from their expressive language mode. The fact that they were able to do this successfully is no small accomplishment. The African slaves were illiterate, in terms of English, which suggest that the Gullah dialect was designed for oral communication. Any attempt, including our effort, to reduce to writing what is captured through oral discourse in Gullah, presents a set of special problems. One of the major problems encountered is that of deciding how to represent graphically many of the Gullah expressions that have no English counterparts. For linguists, that problem can be solved often by phonemic transcription. However, this solution is practical only when words have generally accepted pronunciations. This is not the case with Gullah. There is a variety of ways to convey a single meaning as well as different pronunciations for the same words. This explains, in part, why Gullah, that has been reduced to a written form, may appear to have many inconsistencies. In spite of the inconsistencies, which we think were by design, Gullah passes the critical test of mutual intelligibility among native speakers of the dialect.

An interesting activity designed to enhance students' or other interested individuals' understanding of "Black English" involves a cooperative effort in code switching. Working cooperatively in small groups, they attempt to translate material presented in variant dialects to "Standard English." The sample exercises below represent ideas taken from an African folktale and presented in a format that utilizes many of the characteristics of one dialect of urban ghetto speech. The same folktale is also presented in Gullah to help emphasize the difference between what is truly Black English and what we prefer to label as Urban Ghetto Speech. The "Standard English" version, which is not a part of the exercise, is included here as a frame of reference.

The Rabbit and the Python

This old snake was waiting patiently for a meal to come his way. Almost all of the little animals kept out of his reach. They have seen the bad things that happened to their friends that got too close. When that old snake grabs you, nobody ever gets away. Now the rabbits, are too fast and tricky for the old snake. But old snake, has already planned how to catch a rabbit and he thinks he's going to do it soon. It might be a long time coming, but he's not going to take no for an answer. He just sits and waits knowing that sooner or later something good is going to happen.

Later that day, the old snake called out from his hole, help help help! Now the rabbit is too smart to fall for that trick. He just hops around waiting to see what's going to happen. Then the field rat came along and stopped to listen. When a field rat finds another animal in trouble, he takes advantage of the situation. The field rat thinks he's going to eat some snake for dinner. But old snake has his own plan. He just sits and waits.

The field rat sneaked to a safe distance from the hole and yelled, come on out so I can help you! Old snake said come on down and help me. I'm not able to see. The field rat eased a little closer to the hole. Then he yelled, you're not trying to trick me are you snake? Old snake said he would never bite the hand that helps him. This time the field rat put his head over the edge of the hole. Moving like lightning, the old snake sank his fangs into the field rat and began to squeeze him tightly until he died. When the field rat stopped breathing, old snake swollowed him head first.

The rabbit was watching every thing that happened. He gave old snake time to finish swollowing and then he asked him a question. Why did you lie to the field rat old snake? Old snake, almost too full to talk, said he knew I was a snake." I am what I am and I'm never going to be anything else."

The Rabbit and the Python - Urban Ghetto Speech Format

"Dis ole snake be wait'n patiently for a meal to come his way. Most all of the little animals been keeping out of his reach. They been done saw what bad things happen to their friends that get too close. When that ole snake grab you, ain't nobody never get away. Now the rabbits, they be too fast and tricky for the ole snake. But ole snake, he done already plan how to catch a rabbit and he be's thinking he gonna do it soon. It might be a long time com'n, but he ain't never gonna take no for a answer. He jus be's sit'n and wait'n knowing that sooner or later something good gonna happen.

Later dat day, the ole snake call out from his hole, he—p he—p he—p! Now the rabbit, he be's too smart to fall for dat trick. He just hop around wait'n to see what gonna happen. Then the field rat come along and stop to listen. When a field rat find another animal in trouble, he be's taking advantage of the situation. The rat thinking he gonna eat some snake for dinner. But ole snake, he got his own plan. He jus be's sit'n and wait'n.

The field rat snuck to a safe distance from the hole and yell, come on out so I can he—p you! Ole snake say come on down and he—p me. I ain't able to see. The field rat ease a bit closer to the hole. Then he yell, you ain't put'n me on is you snake? Ole snake say he ain't never gonna bite the hand that he—p him. This time the field rat put his head over the edge of the hole. Moving like lightning, the ole snake sink his fangs into the field rat and put him in a tight squeeze til he die. Then he swollow him head first.

The rabbit be's watch'n every thing that went down. He give ole snake time to finish swollowing and then he ask him a question. Why you lie to the field rat ole snake? Ole snake, almost too full to talk, say he been done knowed I was a snake." I is what I is and I ain't never gonna be nothing else.

De Rabid an de Snek – Gullah Format

De ole snek beena wait dey clean to dey don fa he meal to com ta he. Mose all creacha beena keep outta he way. Dey beena kno bad ting appened ta dey wha git ta close. Wen dat ole snek beena grab ya, don no body beena eber git loose. De ole rabid don beena ta fas and tricky fa de ole snek. But dat dey ole snek beena tricky; he plan fa ketch dat rabid fa sho. E donna kno da time no de dey. But he beena kno e no gwine tek kno fa ansa. E jus wait rown fa he time fa com. Fa he kno fa sho he time gwine com.

Now down in da dey, de ole snek beena holla from he hole louda and louda. Dat dey ole rabid beena ta cricky fa dat dey ole snek. E jus hops rown fa see wha gwine fa appen. De ole feel rat been com rown fa stop an lisen. Oona kno no feel rat gwine fa trouble hesef fa no ting less he gwine git sa'in fa he trouble. De feel rat plan fa ketch snek fa dinna. But de ole snek make e own plan. E donna sit an e donna wait.

De feel rat don git back way from da hole, den hollad at de snek an don said fa he ta com out ob da hole so dat he kuud hep he. Ole snek say me caint see ya. De feel rat moov close op ta da hole. Den de rat beena holla ta da snek, oona try fa be tricky wit we. De ole snek say, fa true, he been no bite de han he beena hep he. Rat don gwine an put he head ta da edge ob dat dey hole. Dat ole tricky snek beena moov crick like da lightnin an don bite da feel rat and don break he bref til he don dead up. Wen da ole rat don stop bref, da ole snek don swollow he head fus.

De rabid don been look on an don saw eby ting wha don appen. Rabid give ole snek time fa finish he meal. Den he ax cresion. Why fa oona story ta da rat? Ole snek, he belly mos full up, he say, he been kno wha I be. Me is wha me gwine be, ain't gwine be nuttin else.

From the suggested activities that follow, you can imagine the number of learning experiences that can be planned around this exercise.

- <u>Suggested Activities</u>

1. Identify the verb forms utilized and substitute the proper tense in "standard English."
2. Identify (verb-defective) sentences or units of meaning from which verbs were omitted. Supply correct "Standard English" verb forms.
3. Identify examples of multiple negation and make the correct "Standard English" substitutions.
4. Identify specific examples of consonant cluster simplification, /l / deletion, intervocalic /r / deletion, final consonant deletion, and the use of "be" or "be's" to denote enduring conditions and "been" to denote conditions that have endured over a long period of time.
5. Complete a sentence-by-sentence analysis and rewrite variant constructions in "standard English."

• It is important to note that four of the five suggested activities are done orally. Valuable learning takes place from these and similar activities. Since communication is based on mutual intelligibility, cross-cultural communication as well as acceptance of differences are facilitated tremendously. The sample activities that follow may be done orally or in writing.

• While there are many variant dialects of American English, identifying the verb tenses used along with their utilization patterns helps in distinguishing one from another.

Habitual Tense

1a. She eats toast for breakfast.
1b. She be's eating toast for breakfast.

2a. He rides the bus to school.
2b. He be's riding the bus to school.

3a. They write letters to the newspaper.
3b. They be writing letters to the newspaper.

Develop a rule for the use of be and be's.

_____

_____

Present Tense

1a. She is eating toast for breakfast.
1b. She eating toast for breakfast.

2a. He is riding the bus to school.
2b. He riding the bus to school.

3a. They are writing letters to the newspaper.
3b. They writing letters to the newspaper.

Develop a rule for the use of the verbs in this tense.

_____

Past Tense

1a. She ate toast for breakfast.
1b. She done ate toast for breakfast.

2a. He rode the bus to school.
2b. He done rode the bus to school.

3a. They wrote letters to the newspaper.
3b. They done wrote letters to the newspaper.

Develop a rule for the use of done in this tense.

Past Participle (Present Perfect)

1a. She has eaten toast for breakfast.
1b. She been done ate toast for breakfast.

2a. He has ridden the bus to school.
2b. He been done rode the bus to school.

3a. They have written letters to the newspaper.
3b. They been done wrote letters to the newspaper.

Develop a rule for the use of been done and the verb form used._____

_____

_____

Future Tense

1a. She will/shall eat toast for breakfast.
1b. She gonna eat toast for breakfast.

2a. He will/shall ride the bus to school.
2b. He gonna ride the bus to school.

3a. They will/shall write letters to the newspaper.
3b. They gonna write letters to the newspaper.

Develop a rule for the use of gonna.

_____

_____

• **Note: This particular dialect has no grammatical equivalents for the Past Perfect and Future Perfect tenses.**

• Using the verb to sing, write two sentences (one in the language of the academy and one in urban ghetto speech) for each of the five tenses used.

Habitual Tense

_____

_____

_____

_____

Present Tense

_____

_____

_____

_____

Past Tense

_____

_____

_____

_____

Past Participle(Present Perfect)

_____

_____

_____

_____

Future Tense

_____

_____

_____

_____

• Supply the principal parts in "Standard English" and in "Urban Ghetto Speech" for each verb given.

Verb	Standard English	Dialect
to sing	sing	be's singing
	sang	done sang
	sung	been done sang
to see	see	be's seeing
	saw	done saw
	seen	been done saw
to swim	_____	_____
	_____	_____
	_____	_____
to drive	_____	_____
	_____	_____
	_____	_____
to run	_____	_____
	_____	_____
	_____	_____

to go   _____   _____
                _____   _____
                _____   _____

to read   _____   _____
                _____   _____
                _____   _____

to teach   _____   _____
                _____   _____
                _____   _____

to ring   _____   _____
                _____   _____
                _____   _____

to dive   _____   _____
                _____   _____
                _____   _____

to take   _____   _____
                _____   _____
                _____   _____

to buy   _____   _____
                _____   _____
                _____   _____

to sell   _____   _____
                _____   _____
                _____   _____

to choose   _____   _____
                _____   _____

- Transpose the following sentences into "Standard English."

1. They been done wrote the poem.

_____

2. He be's sleeping in his socks.

_____

3. She playing golf.

_____

4. They gonna eat dinner outside.

_____

5. The fat lady been done sang.

_____

6. He done made me mad.

_____

7. She be's dancing in the street.

_____

8. They be diving off the high board.

_____

9. The dog been done ran away.

_____

10. He shooting pool.

_____

11. She done made a cake.

_____

12. They gonna sing soon.

_____

Defending the use of strategies that acknowledge the existence of "Black English" should not be necessary. Unfortunately, there are teachers and administrators who have not reached a level of enlightenment that supports taking full advantage of what students already know. Probably its best defense is presented by students through their enthusiastic participation, their cooperative approach to learning, and their increased learning outcomes.

In one chapter of Ralph Ellison's *Invisible Man,* a native's poignant suggestion to a teacher who questioned his motivation to achieve, may be paraphrased in the following manner: Yes teacher, I can learn and if you allow me to hold on to what 's mine . . . not only will I learn, but I will teach you how to make the desert bear fruit. The implications this holds for teachers working with culturally diverse student populations ought to be clear.

One of the major impediments for Blacks attending our public schools is related to language acquisition. This is particularly true for those whose primary speech patterns consist of Urban Ghetto Speech. Speakers of many of those variant dialects of English are treated by teachers in a manner that causes them to avoid interacting altogether. When this occurs, not only does language acquisition suffer, but learning, in general, has been jeopardized. Teaching, when reduced to its essence, is interaction that facilitates learning. This should suggest to both teachers and parents that if you can't interact with children, you can't teach them.

Earlier in this writing, we highlighted some of the similarities and differences existing between the Gullah dialect (the original Black English) and Urban Ghetto Speech. One of the distinctions we made suggested that a major difference between the two is that the Gullah people constructed language by intermingling west African words with English, French, German, Scottish Gaelic, Spanish, and Portuguese. Additionally, they created phonologically similar substitutes for existing English words to produce units of meaning. This confluence of many different languages to produce a means of oral communication, that satisfied the requirement for mutual intelligibility among the Gullah people, was a remarkable fete. That fete is even more remarkable when one considers the circumstances under which it was accomplished. Urban Ghetto Speech reconstructs language by using existing English words in different syntactical configurations and by creating others. The concept of language reconstruction is the defining element of Urban Ghetto Speech. Let's examine that concept more thoroughly. An ideal place to start is with the definition of <u>word</u>.

Linguistically defined, a <u>word</u> is a group of phonemes pronounced without juncture and having <u>a</u> (one) meaning. Obviously, this definition raises questions about the concept of multiple meanings. Linguists suggest that to perceive a word as having multiple meanings is to destroy the notion of word itself. They maintain that the meaning of a word , irrespective of its pronunciation and spelling, serves to distinguish that word from all others. In order to facilitate understanding of this concept, the problem of homophony must be resolved.

<u>Homophones</u> are words having the same sound but different meanings. They are easily recognized as such in the words, <u>to</u>, <u>too</u>, and <u>two</u>, because their spellings are different. However, in the following sentences, three homophones with identical spellings are being used.

- An elephant breathes through its <u>trunk</u>.
- This bark came from the <u>trunk</u> of the tree.
- The luggage was placed in the <u>trunk</u> of the automobile.

These words, <u>trunk</u>, <u>trunk</u>, and <u>trunk</u>, each a homophone of the others, are different words because they have different meanings. Getting students and teachers to accept this particular concept is complicated by the fact that dictionaries list many meanings under one entry rather than rewrite the entry for each meaning. However, there are some strategies that help promote understanding of this concept. One of the most convincing strategies utilizes the proposition of identical qualities. This proposition suggests that words that are identical should be able to accommodate identical affixes. Let's examine the following sentences:

- The bell will <u>ring</u> soon.
- This <u>ring</u> is too large for my finger.

Analysis: The word <u>ring</u> used in the first sentence can accommodate the suffix /-ing/. Our original sentence would then read: The bell will be <u>ringing</u> soon. This is not the case for the word <u>ring</u> used in the second sentence. Clearly they are different words. Once teachers and students begin to look at words from this perspective, many of them will feel that they are gaining a much better understanding of the language. At this point, the influence of Gullah and Urban Ghetto Speech on "Standard English" becomes more easily discernible. The list of words and phrases in Figure 2 are African-American creations. The fact that they have the same sound and the same spelling of other English words does not make them the same words with new meanings. If the meanings are different, the words are different. Figure 2 is provided to demonstrate how Urban Ghetto Speech contributed significantly to the lexicon of "Standard English." The fact that this has been accomplished by using homophones of existing English words eliminated any problems surrounding their graphic representations (spelling).

Examples of Contributions from Urban Ghetto Speech to the "Standard English" Lexicon

pad	(house)	chick	(young lady)
short	(automobile)	Clean	(well dressed)
blood	(a black person)	hawk	(strong wind)
boss	(exceptional quality)	hog	(a car)
dig	(to understand)	rags	(clothes)
dough	(money)	square	(lame)
bread	(money)	fresh	(good looking)
cat	(man)	bad	(good)
cabbage	(money)	natural	(hair style)

Figure 2

Taking full advantage of what students already know is one of the most powerful teaching strategies in existence. The mere understanding of that fact provides strong justification for using the knowledge possessed by native speakers of Urban Ghetto Speech as a vital part of their language instruction. Getting students from where they are to where they ought to be is facilitated tremendously when it is accomplished through having them build on what they already know. However, for this strategy to work successfully, educators must possess a working knowledge of Urban Ghetto

Speech.

The pedagogically sound approach to language instruction for native speakers of Urban Ghetto Speech, described in Part 4 of this effort , pays tremendous dividends.   Recognition of this fact was the driving force behind Dr. Carolyn Gertridge's courageous leadership with the Oakland Unified School District.   In December, 1996, Dr. Gertridge persuaded the Oakland, California Board of Education to adopt the "Ebonics" resolution.   Although the resolution was adopted, the national debate that followed resulted in its emasculation.   The residual of Gertridge's gallant effort holds forth little promise of producing dramatic gains for African-Americans.   Not only did the action taken by the Board ensure a reduced pace of learning, it also chipped away at increasingly more fragile 1st Admendment rights. We are suggesting that this happened because there are people in positions of power who feel threatened by the notion of adequately educating African-Americans.

This section was written specifically to lend assistance to parents and teachers in utilizing what children already know to help them acquire the skills you want them to learn. While it makes no claim of representing research, it offers lucid conceptualizations along with a pedagogically sound and aesthetically appealing approach for working with speakers of variant dialects of English.   This intervention, when thoroughly understood and intelligently applied, results in substantial academic gains for all students. Its most promising attribute may be the potential to produce incredible results in a comparatively short period of time.

Part 5

Some Final Comments

Axiology, the study of values and valuing, is an area for which historians, who have written abridged accounts of Gullah history, have demonstrated little interest. However, the influence of the Gullah culture on the development of many African-American values and lifeways should not be overlooked.

Our ancestors, many of whom were farmers and fisherman, before their forced exodus from Africa, managed their time much differently from the long grueling days required of them by slave masters and overseers. Because Africa provided a climate that was conducive for fishing and for the growing of rice and many other crops throughout the year, the Africans became skillful at proportioning their work so that it would be equally distributed over time. More importantly, the absence of growing seasons, which are typical of American crops, eliminated the need for precise planting and harvesting times. In Africa, all of this was accomplished efficiently and in a manner that interspersed work with relaxation. It is safe to say that how time was perceived and valued by Africans differed significantly from how it was perceived by slave masters and overseers. From the slave masters' perspective, slaves were seen as being lazy, shiftless and not dependable for exhibiting behaviors that showed little regard for punctuality. The major difference between the valuing of time by slaves and slave owners was that the owners ordered their lives around events, and the slaves were accustomed to ordering their participation in events around their lives.

This difference in how time is perceived by many African-

Americans gave rise to the concept of CPT(Colored People's Time). While this concept has a pejorative connotation, it emanated from learned behavior that served Africans well. Contrary to popular belief, it does not mean being consistently late. It means simply that the lives of many African-Americans are not ordered around events. This should suggest their conscious effort to base decisions about the importance of punctuality on a careful analysis of its benefits and consequences. This does not mean its complete disregard. The results of this kind of analyses are reflected in sometimes being early, sometimes being punctual, and sometimes being late. It is their attempt to control rather than be controlled by events. When analyzed from this perspective, it becomes an important component of a sound philosophy of life.

The influence of Gullah, perceived not only as a language or dialect but also as a culture, is a major component of African-Americans' quest for social justice. The progress made thus far toward that end has been truly remarkable. As that quest continues, all African-Americans must realize that forces, created specifically to prevent it from ever reaching full fruition, are firmly implanted. As a result of these conscious efforts to impede the progress of African-Americans, the quest has, of necessity, become a struggle to counteract that conspiracy.

The Gullah culture gave rise to a set of enduring values and some instructive rules for living together harmoniously in a hostile environment. Much of the indignation the Gullah suffered resulted from an expressed belief of their masters and overseers which characterized slaves as being less than human. Only after passage of the 13th and 14th Amendments to the Bill of Rights were African-Americans afforded any constitutional protection. As we approach the year 2000, 1st Amendment rights remain as African-Americans' most precious guardian of freedom. Our argument for making the 1st Amendment rights critical to our survival is not to diminish the importance of the other rights guaranteed us by the Constitution, but to suggest emphatically that if 1st Amendment rights are ever lost, we won't know when we lose the others.

The fabric of the Gullah culture created, in individuals and groups, an incredible resiliency that was physically and emotionally life sustaining. Living in, but never accepting, the conditions of bondage fortified that resiliency in them and in their offspring for generations to come. They survived and flourished, in part, because they knew their survival depended upon a successful struggle. While contemporary African-Americans retained much of that resiliency, far too many have lost sight of the fact that the struggle for survival must continue. Because the rules have changed, the need for the struggle is not as obvious to some as it once was. Although no longer would a Governor dare to block the entrance to a state university, similar results are achieved through more subtle means. However, there can be no mistaking the fact that the major battles will be fought in efforts to achieve equity and excellence in education.

Public education is an area in which the conspiracy has been most effective. The fact that a large segment of the African-American population remains inadequately educated is not a result of insufficient resources being allocated to schools, but rather of an elaborate design to provide them with inferior learning outcomes. As disquieting as the notion of a conspiracy to ensure African-American underachievement may be, an understanding of just how insidious institutional racism has become makes the theory more credible. This is not an indictment against educators, but rather against those who control the education enterprise. Our indictment is leveled against those power brokers whose behavior is based on a recognition of the following fact. **One of the most effective ways for oppressors to maintain dominance over the oppressed is to maintain control of their education.**

There are those who will dismiss this conspiracy theory solely on economic grounds. They will argue that of the approximately one million young people, who drop out of school each year, most are only marginally literate and virtually unemployable. The Committee on Economic Development reports that each year's class of drop-outs costs the nation in excess of $240 billion in crime, welfare, health care, and other services. For every $1.00 spent on education, we spend more than $9.00 to provide services to school drop-outs. About 80% of all prison inmates are school drop-outs. Each inmate costs this country in excess of $28,000 a year. Even those with only a passing interest in American education can see this, and similar arguments, as being philosophically sound.

Our response to those individuals or groups is to admit openly that the continuing cycle of African-American under-achievement diminishes the quality of life for all Americans. However, the "power brokers" have decided that sharing the cost, of providing services for those who are under educated, is a small price to pay for maintaining the advantages and the unearned benefits they now enjoy.

In spite of the fact that most urban school districts have launched special initiatives, which focus on improving academic performances for African-Americans, Latinos, and the poor, regardless of their ethnic background, significant gains have not been made. Even more distressing is the knowledge that many successful teachers of these groups, who labor relentlessly devising strategies that work and speak passionately and convincingly about the benefits for children that accrue from their use, have been excluded from the dialogue on education reform. We're suggesting that this systematic exclusion did not evolve spontaneously, but rather, through a well-crafted design.

In an attempt to lend credibility to the conspiracy theory, we will present some widely-embraced, but ill-advised, policy decisions and questionable practices that have a negative impact on African-American students' achievement. Whether these policy decisions and practices are, in fact, part of a conspiracy, or whether they are simply conspiratorial in nature, the intolerable results are the same. However, the very fact that these ill-advised policies and debilitating practices can survive the scrutiny to which public education is subjected, enhances the plausibility of the existence of a conspiracy. Confirming evidence, for us, is the absence of any serious and sustained challenges to the threshold conditions that allow these practices to continue. In the discussion that follows, we will offer several actual examples of the many educational practices that limit opportunities to learn for African-Americans.

An important mission of any system of education is that of transmitting culture. The commitment of public education toward accomplishing that goal can be measured in terms of which cultures are thought to be worthy of a place in the curriculum. It is clear, by the magnitude of the omissions, that African-American history and culture have not occupied positions of prominence in American schools. To compensate for that shortcoming, more endeavors like this one need to be undertaken. Only then will our children understand a culturally significant meaning of "the grapevine" as having been an important conduit for disseminating information within and among slaves communities rather than as a commercial for California raisins or a Marvin Gaye composition.

The 1954 Supreme Court decision, that overturned the doctrine of "Separate but Equal," was an important victory for African-Americans. In addition to ending segregation in public accommodations, the Court ordered the desegregation of public schools with all deliberate speed. This decision allowed the parents of minority students to choose between sending their children to their segregated home schools or to enroll them in previously all-white neighborhood schools. The "power brokers" recognized immediately that their control over the education of African-Americans was diminished by that decision. However, their control was reestablished quickly through the federal court's desegregation order which introduced forced busing to achieve racial balance. The loss of freedom to choose was the beginning of the demise of education for African-Americans.

The practice of uprooting students from the psychological security provided by their home schools and busing them to areas where they are not welcomed, flies in the face of everything we know about how children learn. Obviously, discontinuing this practice would increase the number of segregated schools throughout the country. However, the position being advanced through this writing is that neighborhood schools, whether integrated or segregated, hold forth the promise of providing an education superior in quality to that provided to any children who are forcibly bussed out of their school communities. This is not to suggest that rescinding court-ordered busing would eliminate the need to continue the struggle for educational equity. It does, however, suggest that the kind of reform needed to improve educational outcomes for minority student populations can prove more effective under those circumstances.

Historically, there have been few opportunities for low-income families and communities of people of color to have their perspectives on education reflected in any kind of reform movements. The fact that these families have not figured prominently in efforts to improve public education may be another reason why many reform movements have not resulted in significant gains for minority students. The voices of minorities are critical in reaching consensus about how to make educational experiences more productive and more empowering for children of color (Delpit, 1988). She maintains that an appropriate education for poor children and children of color can be devised only in consultation with adults who share their culture. Black parents, educators of color, and members of poor communities must be allowed to participate fully in the discussion of what kind of instruction is in their children's best interest.

There is emerging literature on the liberatory pedagogy of successful teachers of African-American children (Delpit, 1992; Foster, 1991; King, 1991; Ladson-Billings, 1994). The literature describes this pedagogical approach as culturally relevant teaching. In contrast with assimilationist teaching, which encourages children to think and act in ways that are consistent with those exhibited by members of the dominant culture in our society, culturally relevant teaching allows African-American children to achieve academic excellence without giving up their cultural identity. Additionally, culturally relevant teaching helps African-American students place their identity in national and global contexts and helps them develop the intellectual and cultural tools to work toward progressive social change (Giroux, 1988; Ladson-Billings and Henry, 1990). An essential component for the success of these innovations is parental and community involvement. This kind of involvement and forced busing to achieve racial balance are mutually exclusive events.

When students are bussed from their own neighborhoods into other school communities, they become marginalized social groups regardless of their racial identities. If they happen to be black and poor, they are likely to exhibit a lack of trust and to feel excluded by the school. The dynamics of these variables relegate academic achievement to a comparatively insignificant position. The results of forced busing limit academic achievement for all children. However, its impact on African-American children is devastating. The knowledge that its consequences far outweigh its benefits is shared by most educators. The fact that this practice has survived, in spite of overwhelming evidence that documents its debilitating influence on all students, particularly African-Americans, suggests that it is part of the conspiracy.

While the Gullah people displayed no obvious signs of gender discrimination, they had the wisdom to separate the sexes when it was thought to be mutually beneficial. The final preparation of adolescents, culminating in rites of passage into adulthood, was one such occasion. The rituals, as well as other important information regarding the responsibilities of adulthood, were taught in single-sex learning arrangements. That practice was maintained because of its effectiveness.

In the United States, as well as in Europe, many all-male and all-female schools have soared to positions of prominence on the strength of their academic programs. Some scholars argue that their generally superior learning outcomes result from eliminating the impact of interactive behaviors between the sexes that are particularly inhibiting for girls. Others maintain that the support structures formed by these single-sex learning arrangements increase motivation to

71

achieve. Regardless of the reasons, there is general agreement on the notion that many of these schools produce extraordinary achievement levels for those in attendance.

Historically, the reason for placing boys and girls in separate learning environments in American schools was to ensure that boys were better educated. Today, the justification for such grouping strategies is to enhance achievement levels for both groups. While there is no convincing evidence to suggest that one sex benefits more than the other from instruction in single-sex classes, girls are more likely to enjoy greater advantages. This is particularly true among certain age groups and with regard to specific subject areas.

The most obvious advantage for girls comes in those curriculum areas where their achievement levels lag significantly behind their male counterparts. The factors very often responsible for this achievement gap are directly related to how boys and girls interact during male-dominated subjects such as math and science. The interaction between boys and girls, particularly adolescents, as well as the differential treatment from teachers, can have a debilitating effect on female achievement levels. This phenomenon sometimes is obscured by the fact that boys achieve a higher level of competence on tests of math and science than girls, but girls often receive better grades on report cards. Single-sex classes mute much of the differential treatment from teachers and all of the male verbal aggressiveness that encourages many females to become passive learners.

Similarly, language arts classes, which are usually dominated by girls, produce a passivity in boys that actually limits their active involvement in the learning process. This suggests that the benefits to accrue from single-sex classes are shared by both boys and girls.

During the 1994-95 school year, the Marsteller Middle School in Manassas, Virginia began to separate some eighth-grade classes by gender. What they hope to accomplish by this bold move is to establish and maintain classroom climates that are more conducive to the success of girls in math

72

and science and boys in the language arts. Because of the promise held forth by this organizational arrangement, the Prince William County School Board voted in April of 95 to allow Marsteller to expand its program to as many as 300 boys and girls for the 1995 - 96 school year. In addition to math and science, some social studies and language arts classes are separated by gender.

However, the program is not without its critics. Some argue that programs, like this one, are in violation of Title IX provisions, which were established to prevent discrimination on the basis of sex. The key to their legal existence, seems to be, the cooperation of students and parents. As long as students do not claim being denied the opportunity to attend coed classes, or being forced to attend sexually segregated classes, this kind of organization can withstand the legal challenges that may be leveled against it.

Another more comprehensive experiment in single-gender classes is being conducted at the Robert W. Coleman Elementary School in Baltimore, Maryland. The principal at Coleman, Mrs. Addie Johnson, speaks both passionately and convincingly about the benefits that accrue to the more than 520 boys and girls involved in the program. Because of the number of innovations existing at Coleman, it is difficult to establish cause and effect regarding a specific intervention. Mrs. Johnson and her staff credit single-gender classes with providing the climate variables that help produce significant increases in math and reading achievement levels. Among the most noteworthy of these were:

- A new work ethic grounded in cooperation and collaboration

- A sense of responsibility among students for helping others achieve success

- A sense of respect for self and others that drastically reduced fighting among students

- A significant reduction in non-task oriented behavior

- An elimination of the negative interaction that can result from cross gender competition

Research on Coleman's innovations is being conducted by the Philadelphia-based Research for Better Schools and Chicago's DePaul University School of Education. While many anxiously await the results of those investigations, there is one preliminary conclusion that can be drawn. After five years of experience with single-gender classes, the school's administration, staff, students, and the surrounding community have agreed that the advantages far outweigh the disadvantages.

While some researchers have expressed concerns regarding single-sex classes, there seems to be universal agreement on their potential to aid in producing superior learning outcomes. Knowledge of that fact alone should be sufficient to ensure greater proliferation of this organizational design. Its use would seem to be particularly helpful to those schools serving large African-American populations. In reality, the schools engaged in the toughest struggles to achieve that elusive goal of equity and excellence in education, are least likely to employ the most promising practices. Let us emphasize again that this is not an indictment against educators, whose efforts to embrace many promising practices are often thwarted. The thought of African-Americans and other children of color achieving at levels commensurate with their potential runs counter to the "power brokers'" vision of education for minorities.

Very exclusive white single-sex academies (both public and private) have existed in this country for years with virtually no challenges to their existence. However, when a group of educators and community members in Milwaukee, Wisconsin wanted to operate an academy for African-American males, the civil libertarians mounted a legal challenge that would not allow the project to get off the ground. The group's original plan, which was not allowed to be implemented, has resulted in the Dr. Martin Luther King, Jr. African-American Immersion Elementary School which also admits African-American females.

A similar fate was suffered by Detroit's Malcolm X, Marcus Garvey, and Paul Robeson Elementary schools. Each was planned to operate as an all-male academy. After legal challenges, each has enrolled girls in its program. New York City's Ujamaa Institute, which was conceived as an all-male academy, is now a coeducational school. It's important to note that many of the challenges to the all-male school concept came from the U.S. Department of Education's Office for Civil Rights. The all-male kindergarten and first grade classes, that operated briefly in Dade County Florida, were ordered by that office to cease operating as single-sex classes in 1989.

What is most troubling about these challenges is that they seem to focus on those institutions that have demonstrated a strong commitment to interrupting the cycle of minority underachievement. The all-male classes at the Matthew A. Henson Elementary School in Baltimore survived the Title IX challenge. Their program survived because of principal Leah Hasty's tenacity which gained the support of the state attorney general's office. This program's survival is truly an exception to the rule.

During the 1995-96 school year, a school in a New Jersey school district reorganized into single-sex classes. According to reports, their well-conceived plan had the support of the superintendent, the community, the school staff, and the students. After operating long enough for several evaluations to be completed, it was clear that their reorganization was working. The incredible gains being made by all students, particularly African-Americans, were attributed to climate variables created by the reorganization. Shortly after the program's success was documented, the district's superintendent received a directive from the New Jersey State Department of Education to discontinue single-sex classes. While it is clear that the directive came through the state department of education, it is just as clear to us that it did not originate there. This scenario suggests the kind of control "power brokers" exert through a well-conceived conspiracy.

As we mentioned earlier in this writing, far too many African-American parents have lost sight of some of the most cherished principles of child rearing embraced by the Gullah. This has resulted in too many children's entering kindergarten at a decided disadvantage, a problem for which public education cannot be held responsible. That responsibility must rest squarely on the shoulders of parents. Our ancestors took advantage of every opportunity presented them to share their knowledge with the youth. The knowledge the Gullah people acquired, before formal systems of education for blacks were in place, came through the grapevine and through life's experiences. However difficult the acquisition of knowledge may have been, the determination to pass it on to others, particulary the young, was an obligation felt by all adults. The scenario that follows demonstrates how youth suffer when that kind of commitment is lacking in parents.

A young mother and her five-year old child entered an elementary school office to register for kindergarten. Part of the registration process included a conference involving the mother, the child, and one of the school's kindergarten teachers. During this conference, the teacher showed the child a picture of an escalator and asked him to name it. The little boy could explain what it was used for, but he didn't know its name. The mother tried to help him put a name to the picture by reminding him how many times they had used it together at the mall. What she did not know, until that brief encounter at school, was how important it was for her to have said to her child at the time they were using it, "This is an escalator." That's an easy thing to do, but because she had not taken the time to do it, her child had lost an important opportunity for learning. Multiply that one occasion by the number of times the "teachable moment" has been lost for African-American children, and the magnitude of the problem is brought more clearly into focus.

While public education must be held harmless for the fact that many minority-culture children enter school at a disadvantage, what happens to them after they enter boarders on inhumane treatment. If much of what has been inflicted upon African-Americans and other minorities through our public schools had been orchestrated by anyone other than

Americans, it would be considered an act of cruelty.

While we believe some of this nations most prominent citizens are supportive of public education in general, they have not displayed a real sense of outrage for what we've managed to accomplish for our minority populations. This absence of moral indignation raises serious questions about the legitimacy of their expressed belief in the need for an educated citizenry. Their actions seem more intent on assisting schools in their expanding role of engineering social reproduction.

A classic example of this kind of subterfuge is presented by Hernstein and Murray in their "best-selling" 1994 book, *The Bell Curve.* In this writing, they describe what they perceives as a permanent underclass of approximately twelve million people whose children are born dumb (intellectually deficient) and therefore, are destined to live and die in poverty. Using this grotesque preception as a sound basis for social policy recommendations, they go on to advocate eliminating funds allocated for Head Start and Title I programs and redirecting them to programs for the gifted and talented. This recommendation would close two of the more viable access routes toward upward mobility for the poor and children of color and help to validate the authors' uninformed prognosis. This book, which was loaded with racist dogma, sold millions of copies. Unfortunately, the lack of public outrage, for the authors' major premise, indicates how comfortable Americans have become with their prejudices. Many Americans, who believe that it is politically incorrect to voice such sentiments publicly, have accepted them privately. The saddest commentary of all is that many legislators as well as educators in policy-making positions embrace such ideas.

The scripts which dictate success or failure for poor children and children of color are not in their genes but rather in the agendas these children either establish or have established for them. Michael Jordan was not born with a basketball in each hand, nor was Dr. Benjamin Carson born holding a scalpel. The rise to prominence for each of them was achieved through dedication, commitment and determination to be the best in their chosen professions. This notion of rising above adversity was a driving force among the Gullah people. It is reinforced constantly in Seymour Fliegel's book, *Miracle in East Harlem* and through the numerous examples of successful individuals who emerged from pockets of poverty throughout the country.

Unfortunately, the education establishment has not yet developed an effective process for identifying and disseminating information about these success stories to those who have a need to know. More importantly, it has not encouraged the development of strategies and techniques that would be instrumental in ensuring their replication. If that ever occurs, we will have a supporting structure for public education that allows those who may be less well informed to stand on the shoulders of giants.

One of the most debilitating practices, affecting those who enter school at a disadvantage, centers around instructional pacing. Accepted practice is based on a philosophy that encourages the spoon feeding of skills to all students who are not learning at the desired rate. What this accomplishes is to slow down the learning process. This philosophy gets reinforced through what is being taught, how it's taught, and the manner in which students are grouped for instruction. The resulting paradigm guarantees that the students demonstrating the greatest need are afforded fewer opportunities to learn.

Another is the crippling practice of inflating the grades of under achievers which ultimately sustains the disgusting concept of social promotions. Equally debilitating for students and teachers is the practice of evaluating elementary students' progress against, what is perceived to be, their instructional levels. This practice, which is used by a number of school systems around the country, disregards grade-level expectations entirely. Students' instructional levels are determined by teachers' assessments of their needs. This means that the progress of a fourth-grade student may be evaluated against how well he or she handles a first, second, or third grade curriculum. This also means that students, who may be three years below grade level, often receive satisfactory grades on their progress reports. Although instructional levels may be indicated clearly on the progress reports, satisfactory grades suggest to parents and to students that their progress is acceptable. As debilitating as this is for students, minorities in particular, it's even more debilitating for teachers. They must live with the guilt of being intellectually dishonest in their evaluation of students' progress. Finally, we want to point out how one increasingly popular effort to improve failing schools, known as reconstitution, often compounds the problems for under achieving students.

The impact of reconstituting schools as a school improvement strategy needs to be examined carefully. That examination should begin with the understanding that most failing schools result from continued use of ill-advised practices rather than from ineffective teachers. Very little is gained if an entire staff is replaced, but ill-advised policy and debilitating practices are maintained. When all the ramifications of the process are considered, its influence on student achievement may be more disabling than enabling. This is particularly true when the process is used as a political expediency rather than a well-planned and skillfully executed school improvement strategy. This happens more often than policy makers care to admit, and the results are usually disastrous.

San Francisco's school district, a pioneer in attempting to improve failing schools by transferring their entire staffs, now wants to retreat from this drastic reform measure. The Board of Education as well as school administration officials are trying to reach some middle ground between those who view reconstitution as the magic bullet and those who see it as a process that exacerbates a situation that is already intolerable. The present superintendent recognizes that the practice stigmatizes schools and creates animosity among teachers.

The national profile for failing schools indicates that each enrolls a high percentage of racial, ethnic, economic, and linguistic minorities. These schools house many of our students with the greatest needs. The real challenge for those relying on reconstitution as a school improvement strategy is to conduct the process in a manner that meets students' needs, avoids stigmatizing the schools involved and minimizes the animosity created among teaching staffs.

There are several ways through which this can be accomplished without alienating many dedicated professionals who have not been successful in creating either the learning environment or students' attitude toward learning that supports improved learning outcomes. A starting point is for those in charge of the operation to recognize and openly admit that successfully teaching the populations of those schools identified for reconstitution requires a set of special skills. Those special skills are not provided through teacher preparation programs. The different experiences of teachers assist in the acquisition of those skills for some and not for others. This should suggest that rarely, if ever, should reconstitution result in the transfer of an entire staff.

Teachers, in general, are adept at recognizing their own weaknesses. Being transferred for not possessing those special skills required for success with a given population should not become the source of any animosity. However, the practice of total-staff transfers invariably includes some teachers who do possess those special skills and are using them effectively. Not having those contributions recognized is a source of legitimate teacher animosity.

This total-staff transfer approach usually results from two separate sets of circumstances or a combination of the two. The first is that the school system involved did not respond effectively to the developing crises while they were still relatively easy to manage. Complaints about these schools from community members, as well as from staff, are often ignored completely or treated in a cavalier manner. This is a calculated risk that the Superintendent is willing to take because minority communities are not likely to mobilize protesters to the extent that a critical mass is developed. As a result, problems continue to mount until crises levels are obvious. At this point, the involvement of outside advocacy groups moves the Superintendent to act. The action taken is, more often than not, an act of political expediency that results in the transfers of the administrative team and the entire teaching staff.

The second set of circumstances revolves around the fact that superintendents, or those responsible for the reconstitution process, have not done their homework. While they have gathered sufficient information documenting the schools' failure, they are not sufficiently knowledgeable regarding the performance of individual teachers. Those teachers who are performing in an exemplary manner should be allowed to feel secure in their positions. This point cannot be overstated. The very fact that a school is identified for reconstitution is evidence that its students are under achieving. When the entire staff is transferred, the magnitude of the school's problems is exaggerated grossly.

Perceptions of the problems, created by the drastic step of transferring the entire staff, are sufficient to discourage successful teachers of culturally diverse populations from applying for a position at these schools. This practically ensures that these schools will be staffed with teachers who have neither the experience nor the expertise required to meet the challenges presented. Those educators who understand that it is the teaching staff that, to a large extent, determines a school's success or failure should be guided by that fact when making staff changes.

The two recommendations being offered here, both of which deal with staff selection and utilization, can have a tremendous impact on students' achievement levels. The first is to place the best and brightest teachers with the students demonstrating the greatest need. In theory, few would disagree with its potential for making a tremendous difference for a substantial number of students. However, many school administrators continue to place their best teachers with their best students. Some school districts even require additional training for their teachers of "gifted" students. The end result, of this rather traditional, but ill-conceived, staffing pattern, is that the students with the greatest need are often placed with teachers that actually limit their opportunities to learn.

The second recommendation emphasizes the advantages of placing black teachers, when possible, with classes having a majority of black students. This is not to suggest that black teachers do a better job of teaching children of color than white teachers. However, there is some evidence that black children are willing to learn more from black teachers than from white teachers (Foster, 1991; King, 1991; Ladson-Billings, 1994). Trust and legitimacy are two conditions for learning that must be satisfied before black children allow themselves to become fully involved in the learning process (Erickson, 1987). These conditions are more likely to be met when children of color interact with black teachers.

As irrefutable evidence of what can be accomplished by poor children of color when their education results from a total community endeavor, we offer an abbreviated case study of the St. Helena Elementary School. With a population in excess of 800 students in classes ranging from pre-kindergarten through fifth grade, the students, staff, and school community have completely destroyed any credibility that may have been associated with a major premise advanced by Hernstein and Murray in their book, The *Bell Curve*. According to their theory as we understand it, the majority of the children born to parents who reside in the Gullah communities of the Sea Islands are born intellectually deficient and, as such, are destined for life-long membership in an illiterate and permanent underclass. Under the tireless and extremely capable leadership of principal, Dr. LaVerne Lebby Davis, the St. Helena Elementary School, with a population that fits the description of "black and poor" has removed another myth from the arsenal of the power brokers.

Approximately 95% of the school's population is African-American, and more than 95% of the total enrollment qualifies for the free and reduced-cost lunch programs. In spite of what many educators would consider to be mitigating circumstances, the school leads Beaufort County in achievement as measured by standardized tests. If this level of academic achievement had been confined to a single school year, it would be considered an anomaly. However, that is clearly not the case. For four of the past five years, this school has been selected as a South Carolina State Incentive Reward Winner. Because of St. Helena Elementary's consistent pursuit of excellence, it was deregulated by the South Carolina State Department of Education. Currently there are only two deregulated schools in the nineteen-school Beaufort County district. A deregulated school is granted increased autonomy in curriculum design and greater flexibility in the delivery of instructional services. South Carolina's State Department of education is to be commended for recognizing that minority educators must be included in the dialogue on education reform.

Dr. Davis is quick to point out that much of what has been accomplished at the St. Helena Elementary school has resulted from a total community endeavor. There are many partnerships with businesses, civic and social organizations, cadres of parent volunteers, and mentors that worked closely with staff during and after school hours toward achieving a common goal. Not only did they believe that they could make a significant difference in achievement levels for under achieving students, they were committed to do whatever was required to transform their desires into reality.

As recently as 1992, the achievement scores for students at St. Helena Elementary were among the lowest in the district. Dr. Davis initiated a relentless pursuit of excellence that rapidly became contagious. Once the level of support for what she wanted to accomplish reached a critical mass, the decision was made to focus on mathematics instruction. In a relatively short period of time, test scores in math for St. Helena's students went from the district's lowest to the highest. On the Metropolitan Achievement Test administered during the 1996-97 school year, St. Helena's first grades scored at the seventy-fifth percentile while second and third grades scored at the eightieth percentile. One of the most significant indicators of how students, who are assumed to be lacking in motivation to achieve by many educators, responded to the rigorous demands placed on them by their teachers, is a daily attendance rate of 99.4%.

While this is but a single example of success, it should be sufficient to destroy many of the myths that perpetuate the cycle of underachievement for African-Americans. If it can happen in a Gullah community on a Sea Island in South Carolina, it can happen everywhere.

As the Sea Islands continue to change, many of the structures that were visible reminders of the Gullah life style have disappeared. The Praise Houses and the slave cabins, that once dotted the landscape, have been reduced to memories. Opportunities to engage in or listen to conversations held in that storied Gullah dialect are diminishing rapidly. However, the contributions made by this fabled people will live on forever. All Americans, regardless of their racial, ethnic, or economic group affiliation, will embrace an array of culturally enriching activities and beliefs that emanated from Gullah. Interests that range from the wearing of braids and dreadlocks, through culturally inspired music and dance steps, to such culinary delights as hog head cheese paté, lend a certain vitality and authenticity to life that cannot be obtained from a sterile European heritage.

This effort to enlighten and to encourage our readers to become more knowledgeable about a vanishing culture has been, for us, a labor of love. We hope that the glimpse into the Gullah culture provided serves as more than a sources of information. We see it serving as a wakeup call for both parents and educators whose efforts toward improving the human condition have not produced the desired results. It was the Gullah experience that gave rise to the "melting pot" notion that has been used as an analogue for a truly integrated society. Out of the Gullah experience, defined by ancestral strength and traditions, came ideas relating to family stability, group solidarity, upward mobility, the importance of education, and the fact that oppression diminishes oppressors along with the oppressed. These powerful statements about life and living are both informative and instructive. While we have provided only a glimpse into the Gullah experience, we've tried to create the understanding that its full appreciation requires that the long trek begun around 1530 be thoroughly understood.

Racism is a form of psychosis that is here to stay. Understanding and accepting that fact should strengthen the resolve of African-Americans to achieve success in spite of its existence. The determination to succeed against overwhelming odds is an important part of the Gullah legacy. However, if we are successful in having our children read, write, and compute at the highest level of proficiency, but have not taught them to understand their history to the extent that they become more mindful of and show more consideration for other human beings, we have failed. That goal can be accomplished. The cause is noble; the purpose is clear, and the time to act is now.

As a parting gesture, we conclude this effort by translating into Gullah the two preceding paragraphs which appear in Italics.

Dis ya ting oona ta do, done been done fa oona's reada bout oona's culcha dat been mose gone, done been done fa we, fa da layba ob oona's lub. Oona da hope dat oona done git wa oona mose need from oona culcha. Oona da kno dat mose ob we been sleep an need fa a waki op ta ting dat mose chaag oona fa betta. It done beena dat Gullah spirance dat maak we all mose same in we siety. Out ob da Gulla spirance, oona done been raise up wit oona famlee an ting, oona ancesta powa, an dat oona mus all da move ta gatha. Oona mose tink dat one hol oona down, done move netha. Dese wuds bout oona's Gulla spirance tis mose bout oona's life an oona's libin, an oona wanz oona fa lurn from dis. But oona da kno oona mus waak wit oona baak oona roun fifteen tirties (1530s) fa oona ta kno bout we.

Dis ya ting bout racism whadda maak mose peopas ta tink dat dey mose betta, maak mose peopas ta tink dat dey da mose cracky. Oona mus kno oona's powa. Oona mus kno leh kno body fa tell oona E kno can fa lurn, an mus do al E can fa do fa E sef an E culcha. Oona mus be laak a fish wha try fa swim op da ribba. It done maak dat dare fish mose strong fa try. We done been like dat ole fish. E done be mose portant in da ribba cause E done fa try haada den da odda fish. Ef oona chillun be da lurn, dey must da lurn who

85

dey be an wha fa dey com from. We mus gib we chillun da ting dat maak dem lub sef an odda peopas or da ting aint gone nebba maak no sens. Dis ya ting is mose big an mose portant ta oona, an dis ya is da time fa oona ta do.

Suggested Reading

Asante, Molefi K. and Mattson, Mark T. *Historical and Cultural Atlas of African-Americans.* New York: Macmillan Publishing Company, 1992.

Bennett, Lerone, Jr. *Before the Mayflower.* New York: Penguin, 1988.

Bergman, Peter. *The Chronological History of the Negro in America.* New York: The New American Library, 1969.

Berlin, Ira. *Slaves Without Masters: The Free Negro in the Antebellum South.* New York: Pantheon, 1974.

Billington, Allen Ray, ed. *The Journal of Charlotte L. Forten.* New York: W. W. Norton & Company, 1981.

Black, J. Gary. *My Friend The Gullah.* Columbia, South Carolina: R. L. Bryan Company, 1974.

Blassingame, John W. *The Slave Community: Plantation Life in the Antebellum South.* 2nd ed., rev. New York: Oxford Press, 1979.

Boles, John B. *Black Southerners, 1619–1869.* Lexington: University Press of Kentucky, 1983.

Campbell, Edward D. C., Jr. and Rice, Kym S., ed. *Before Freedom Came: African-American Life in the Antebellum South.* Richmond: The Museum of the Confederacy and the University Press of Virginia, Charlottesville, 1991.

Creel, Margaret Washington. *A Peculiar People: Slave Religion and Community Culture Among the Gullahs.* New York: New York University Press, 1988.

Elkins, Stanley M. *Slavery: A Problem in American Institutional and Intellectual Life.* 3rd ed. Chicago: University of Chicago Press, 1976.

Faust, Drew Gilpin, ed. *The Ideology of Slavery: Pro-slavery Thoughts in the Antebellum South, 1830–1860.* Baton Rouge: Louisiana State University Press, 1981.

Fishel, Leslie H., Jr. and Quarles, Benjamin. *Negro American, A Documentary History.* Glenview, Illinois: Scott, Foresman and Company, 1967.

Franklin, John Hope. *From Slavery to Freedom: A history of Negro Americans.* New York: Alfred A. Knopf, 1974.

Genovese, Eugene D. *Roll, Jordan, Roll: The World the Slaves Made.* New York: Pantheon, 1974.

Green, Jonathan. *Gullah Images: The Art of Jonathan Green.* Columbia, South Carolina: University of South Carolina Press, 1996.

Higgenbotham, A. Leon, Jr. *In the Matter of Color, Race and the American Legal Process –the Colonial Period.* New York: Oxford University Press, 1978.

Higgins, Chester, Jr. and Coombs, Orde. *Some Time Ago, A Historical Portrait of Black Americans, 1850–1950.* Garden City, New York: Anchor Press/Doubleday, 1980.

Jones, Howard. *Mutiny on the Amistad: The Saga of a Slave Revolt and Its Impact on American Abolition, Law, and Diplomacy.* New York: Oxford University Press, 1987.

Jordan, Winthrop D.*White Over Black: American Attitudes Toward the Negro, 1550–1812.* Chapel Hill: University of NC Press, 1968.

Joyner, Charles W. *Down by the Riverside: A South Carolina Slave Community.* Urbana: University of Illinois Press, 1984.

Kinlaw-Ross, Eleanor. *Dat Gullah and Other Geechie Traditions.* Atlanta: Crick Edge Productions, 1996.

Woodson, Carter G. *The Mis-Education of the Negro.* Washington, D.C.: Africa World Press, Inc., 1990.